# The SIMS 2

## NIGHTLIFE
### EXPANSION PACK*

## PRIMA Official Game Guide

### GREG KRAMER

Prima Games
A Division of Random House, Inc.

3000 Lava Ridge Court, Ste. 100
Roseville, CA 95661
1-800-733-3000
www.primagames.com

*The Sims™ 2 or The Sims™ 2 Special DVD Version is required to play The Sims™ 2 Nightlife.

# The Sims 2 nightlife
## EXPANSION PACK

PRIMA GAMES

The Prima Games logo is a registered trademark of Random House, Inc., registered in the United States and other countries. Primagames.com is a registered trademark of Random House, Inc, registered in the United States. Prima Games is a division of Random House, Inc.

Product Manager: Jill Hinckley
Editor: Alaina Yee

Please be advised that the ESRB Ratings icons, "EC", "E", "E10+", "T", "M", "AO", and "RP" are trademarks owned by the Entertainment Software Association, and may only be used with their permission and authority. For information regarding whether a product has been rated by the ESRB, please visit www.esrb.org. For permission to use the Ratings icons, please contact the ESA at esrblicenseinfo.com.

**Important:**
Prima Games has made every effort to determine that the information contained in this book is accurate. However, the publisher makes no warranty, either expressed or implied, as to the accuracy, effectiveness, or completeness of the material in this book; nor does the publisher assume liability for damages, either incidental or consequential, that may result from using the information in this book. The publisher cannot provide information regarding game play, hints and strategies, or problems with hardware or software. Questions should be directed to the support numbers provided by the game and device manufacturers in their documentation. Some game tricks require precise timing and may require repeated attempts before the desired result is achieved.

ISBN: 0-7615-5145-X

Library of Congress Catalog Card Number: 2005904206

Printed in the United States of America

05 06 07 08 GG 10 9 8 7 6 5 4 3 2 1

# TABLE OF CONTENTS

# Chapter 1

# WHAT'S NEW IN THE SIMS 2 NIGHTLIFE

They say nighttime is the right time, that the night belongs to lovers, that the night is magic. Now, for your Sims, it's all those things and more. Heck, it doesn't even have to be nighttime for some nightlife with the happenin' expansion that is *The Sims 2 Nightlife*.

Sims have always loved to go out on the town, but they've never been able to hang for real with more than one other Sim from their own household. Plus, even when your Sim and his pal arrived at their destination, the companion would go about her own business without much regard for the "Sim what brung her."

With *The Sims 2 Nightlife*, Sims can go out in cohesive groups either casually or on scored group outings or romantic one-on-one dates that can gain your Sim a myriad of benefits. Sims also exhibit attraction to Sims who are their "type," making the courtship game more challenging and interesting than ever. Combine these two new major elements with new Aspirations, objects, social interaction, NPCs, and relationships, and you'll see a whole new world emerge from your Sims' neighborhoods.

So take your Sims downtown or let them enjoy their new powers in their own burgs. Either way, many new adventures and mysteries await them in the neon glow of the night.

Here are but a few of the new features and additions:

◆ New Attraction system allows Sims to build relationships faster with other Sims who suit their particular taste.

◆ A new Chemistry Simology panel displays your Sim's Turn Ons and Turn Off and offers a Chemistry sort for the Relationship panel that shows only Sims to whom your Sim is attracted.

◆ Sims can go on dates with individual Sims to quickly build romance and earn romantic rewards.

◆ Sims can invite several Sims out on the town or to their home with one phone call, thanks to the new group system. Groups stick together and have fun en masse.

◆ Groups can gather for a good time at your Sim's house or on a Community Lot just for fun or on a scored "outing" that earns your Sim valuable rewards.

◆ A new restaurant system offers realistic dining experiences.

◆ Sims can own cars to travel to and from work or school or to Community Lots. No more waiting for cabs and living at the mercy of the carpool.

◆ Sims' lives can be pointed in new directions with the Pleasure Aspiration. And, if they're unlucky enough to misuse a certain object, they could end up with a decidedly odd and awkward new Aspiration. Let's just say, we hope you *really* like grilled cheese.

◆ Sims can become creatures of the night thanks to the arrival of the Grand Vampires in Downtown Community Lots. Being a Vamp limits your daylight activities but offers major benefits after nightfall.

◆ New places for public WooHoo include your Sims' very own cars and the barely private photo booths.

◆ No misdeed goes unpunished now that Sims can harbor grudges. Certain affronts will render a Sim "furious" and uninterested in dealing with the offending Sim for a time.

◆ Almost any object can be placed in your Sims' expanded personal inventories. Want your Sim to pocket a tree? Go right ahead.

# WHAT'S NEW IN *THE SIMS 2 NIGHTLIFE*

◆ Sims can interact with several new NPCs: the Gypsy Matchmaker, the restaurant Host and Server, the Grand Vampires, the Diva, Mr. Big, and the Slob, as well as the eternally disapproving Mrs. Crumplebottom.

◆ Graves can now be moved from the place of their demise to Community Lots or even other family lots (though the ghosts may not be happy about the latter).

◆ Nearby neighboring houses are visible from every lot. You can even switch to a house next door or go directly to the Community Lot across the street without going to the Neighborhood view.

◆ Choosing a Community Lot is now easier thanks to a revamped destination selection tool.

◆ New objects for your home or Community Lots can turn any lot into a nightclub, restaurant, or any happenin' hang out you can imagine.

◆ A new Aspiration reward object can change your Sim's Aspiration, Turn Off, or Turn Ons. Use it at the wrong time, however, and you could get a Sim with an unseemly desire for grilled cheese sandwiches.

◆ New diversions include karaoke machines, bowling alleys, and card tables.

◆ Cover your Sims' floors with a bevy of new rugs.

◆ Seating options expand with modular sectional sofas and curved kitchen islands.

◆ New socials allow for effective outings and dates and for finding the Sims to whom your Sim is most attracted. Discover new nested socials to do while slow dancing, sitting in restaurant booths, and dining.

◆ Discover other Sims' wants, fears, interests, zodiac sign, skills, job, wealth, Turn Ons, and Turn Offs with an array of new Ask socials.

◆ The outfit-planning interface has been revamped to be easier to use.

◆ Your Sims can now cook Crepes Suzette in their very own kitchens. Plus, several new dishes await the culinarily adventurous in restaurants.

◆ New Build mode features include non-rectangular pools, 1/2 walls, several new very big and very small lot sizes, a terrain smoothing tool, garages and driveways, eyedropper-enabled fences, and (via a handy cheat) modifiable roof pitch.

◆ The Lots and Houses Bin has been changed so that unoccupied houses pulled from it remain in the bin to be placed again and again if you desire.

◆ Your custom neighborhoods can be surfaced with two new terrain types: dirt and concrete.

◆ The downtown neighborhood is a destination for all the Sims of your base neighborhoods. You can even start new households or move old ones right in the heart of the electrifying downtown. When you've sampled everything the first downtown has to offer, try your hand at building your own.

# Chapter 2

# DOWNTOWN AND SUNDRY NEW FEATURES

Downtown can be a scary place, but it can also be viscerally exciting–a place that bursts with energy, opportunity, and promise. Sure you might end up with pale skin, fangs, and a taste for Sim-biting, but isn't a good smustle worth the risk?

This chapter provides an overview of how this new kind of neighborhood functions and how it alters life for your Sims old and new. Next, it details several of this expansion pack's extremely important but more compact changes and additions, including the fully enabled personal inventory, new lot navigation tools, and a new way to rid your lot of ghosts.

## The Structure of Downtown

The first time you open one of your base neighborhoods or press the Downtown Chooser button in the upper left corner, you can associate an existing downtown or create a new one.

Downtown neighborhoods (or "nightlife destinations") exist as offshoots of your game's base neighborhoods (Pleasantview, Strangetown, etc.). In other words, any single version of a downtown neighborhood you play is tied exclusively to one of your base neighborhoods and has no connection to other base neighborhoods.

### note

To clear up any confusion, the new kind of neighborhood introduced in *The Sims 2 Nightlife* is called a "downtown" or a "nightlife destination."

The Maxis-designed nightlife destination that ships with your expansion pack is likewise named "Downtown."

This can lead to some confusion, so this guide will refer to nightlife destinations generically as "downtowns" (with a lowercase "d") and the Downtown nightlife destination specifically with a capital "D."

Once a downtown is associated, the full Downtown Chooser appears listing any associated downtowns and a button for creating new downtowns of your own design.

Sims from other base neighborhoods, therefore, don't exist in a downtown even if the same downtown is also associated with other base neighborhoods. In other words, downtowns exist in sort of an urban parallel universe. For example, if both Pleasantview and Strangetown are associated with the Maxis-designed nightlife destination "Downtown," the Smith family will never be seen wandering the lots of Pleasantview's Downtown and the Caliente sisters won't be caught dead (or even undead) in the Strangetown's Downtown.

# DOWNTOWN AND SUNDRY NEW FEATURES

Click on a downtown and you'll see its preview pane.

This is why you must begin the life of any downtown by associating your base neighborhood with it. *The Sims 2 Nightlife* comes complete with one very densely featured downtown and the ability to create any others you wish.

Once you add custom downtowns, they appear alongside any existing downtowns.

# Base and Downtown Neighborhoods: How Do They Relate?

Functionally, base and downtown neighborhoods aren't all that different.

## note

Though they mostly function the same, the Maxis-designed downtown that came with your expansion pack ("Downtown") is very different from the base neighborhoods in terms of design and the number and features of its Community Lots.

♦ Sims can live in downtown neighborhoods just as they can in base neighborhoods.

♦ Downtowns share Lots and Houses and Sim Bins with their base neighborhood, allowing families to move from one to the other and maintain their relationships.

♦ Sims who are met in a downtown neighborhood can be invited over, added to a group, or called for a date or outing by a Sim who resides in the base neighborhood (and vice versa).

♦ Teen Sims residing in a downtown neighborhood are eligible to attend college at any of the base neighborhood's associated universities (if you have the *The Sims 2 University* expansion pack installed, that is).

Special downtown NPCs such as the Grand Vampire appear only in downtown Community Lots.

There are, however, some differences you should be aware of:

♦ The Grand Vampires, the Diva, Mr. Big, and the Slobs (see Chapter 8) appear automatically only in downtown neighborhood Community Lots. Once met, they can be invited, called, or dated just like any other townie.

♦ The generic townies that populate downtown neighborhoods ("downtownies") have more money, better jobs, and higher skills.

♦ In Neighborhood view, downtown neighborhoods are always shown at nighttime (unless, of course, you press the Day/Night toggle button).

It's always nighttime downtown. Well, that's not true, but it looks that way in the Neighborhood view.

 **note**
Though the Grand Vampires appear only randomly downtown, vampirism can spread to your base neighborhood. If a base neighborhood resident invites a downtown vampire to a party or on a visit, outing, or date, your Sim or (if you've already had one of your Sims bitten) any other Sims present with whom the vampire has built relationship will be ripe for the biting. These new vamps can increase their numbers by biting other base neighborhood Sims (and so on but only up to a point). For more on vampires, see Chapter 10.

If the neighboring lot is a Community Lot, the Sim(s) you're currently playing can travel directly to the lot without having to select the Community Lot from the list.

**note**
If a neighboring lot is unoccupied, you can't switch to it.

## Neighboring Lots

No longer is your Sim's lot an island in a sea of nothingness. With the *The Sims 2 Nightlife* expansion pack, everything beyond your Sim's lot is not only visible but also interactive.

Want to switch to a nearby household? No need to exit to the Neighborhood view; just click on any house visible from your Sim's lot and you'll have the option to play it instead.

From any lot, you can now see neighboring residential and Community Lots, streets, and landmarks. Is your Sim's house right next to the power lines? Well, now you can see them from within the lot. How far you can see and in what kind of detail depends on your computer hardware, so play with the settings in the Game Options menu under "Lot View Options."

Those lots around your Sim's house aren't just for decoration, you know. You can, in fact, navigate directly to any visible lot (without having to exit to the Neighborhood view) by clicking on the destination. If the lot is residential, you can choose to switch to playing that lot. If it's commercial, the currently selected Sim can drive or summon a cab automatically (or go to their personal car) and head directly to it.

 **note**
You can turn off this feature by switching off Clickable Neighbors in the Game Options menu.

## Moveable Graves

In the past, when a Sim died, his or her final resting place was the lot on which he or she expired. As long as that tombstone or urn remained on the lot, the deceased's spirit could wander the lot at night, haunt it, and scare residents and visitors. The survivors could either simply suffer these manifestations or unceremoniously sell the memorial marker.

# DOWNTOWN AND SUNDRY NEW FEATURES

With *The Sims 2 Nightlife*, there's another option: move the tombstone/urn to another lot. Markers can be moved to any Community Lot in the base neighborhood, any downtown neighborhood, or college town. They can also be moved to any residential lot but there are some serious logistical requirements and pitfalls to this strategy.

## Moving Graves to Community Lot

To move a grave, click on the marker (tombstone or urn), select Move This Grave, and choose its new resting place.

To move a grave to a Community Lot, click on the grave and select Move This Grave (or Move All Graves if you want to move all the markers on the lot at once). The new standard lot navigation window appears permitting you to select any Community Lot in the base neighborhood or any associated downtowns or college towns.

The marker disappears in a puff of smoke and the grave's owner waves so long.

The deceased makes a brief appearance to wave good-bye, then the ghost and the marker are spirited away to their new resting place. To make this change permanent, you **must** save the lot. If you depart without saving, the grave will return to its place.

When you next visit the selected Community Lot, the marker has been placed there in a random location near the public phone. After nightfall, the dead Sim's ghost may be seen wandering, though it should be a relatively benign haunter.

### notes
To situate it more precisely, click on the tombstone and place it in your inventory. Of course, you can't access your inventory on a Community Lot, so replace the grave by clicking on an open bit of ground and selecting Put Grave Here.

Normally, a ghost would be angry (and, thus, a more aggressive haunter) if there were no family members living on the same lot as his grave. A ghost on a Community Lot harbors no such grudge.

### notes
Ghosts angry for reasons having nothing to do with their old households or families, however, may still be angry ghosts when moved to a Community Lot. Sims who died of hunger, for example, become angry if there's an empty refrigerator (or none at all) on the lot. If the Community Lot lacks available food, starved ghosts haunt at a more intense level.

### note

If, after moving a grave to a Community Lot, you want to delete it entirely, there is a way. From Neighborhood view, enter the Community Lot in Build mode (in other words, directly rather than by having a Sim visit) and "sell" the marker in the normal fashion. You won't get any money for the marker this way but at least the loved one will be put completely to rest.

Alternately, a Sim leaving a lot for a new home may move the grave marker to a new residential lot by putting it in his inventory. Note, however, that unless there is at least one blood relative residing on the new lot, the ghost will haunt its new home at a more aggressive level.

## Plan Outfit Interface

The new Plan Outfit interface is easier to navigate.

The Plan Outfit interface has been revamped and simplified to match the Clothes Shopping interface.

## New Cook-At-Home Food: Crepes Suzette

Home chefs with cooking skill of 7 or higher can make a spectacular new dessert during lunch and dinner hours: Crepes Suzette.

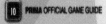
Crepes are a spectacular new dessert food for your Sims to cook at home.

Note that like Baked Alaska, crepes can be dangerous to more than just your Sims' waist-lines. Just before serving, the dish is set aflame. Depending on the skill of the cook, therefore, these sweet treats are served with a chance of self-immolation.

## Inventory

For anyone who's wanted to see what Sims keep in their pockets, the new personal inventory is just the thing.

### note

The inventory was actually introduced with the *University* expansion pack but it wasn't interactive. It only held personal electronics and you couldn't drag anything out of or into it.

Most anything can go in your Sim's personal inventory and anything placed in it can be transferred back into the world.

# DOWNTOWN AND SUNDRY NEW FEATURES

Every Sim has her individual inventory, accessed under the Rewards menu. To place things in it, select the Inventory button and drag an object from the lot into the panel. To deposit things in the world, open inventory and drag items out of it.

**note**

As with the Career and Aspiration Reward menus, opening your Sim's inventory pauses the game.

All objects can be placed in your inventory except:

- Ashes
- Bills
- Buffet table
- Cockroach carcasses
- Dirty dishes
- Doors
- Driveway pieces
- Fireplaces
- Food
- Food dishes and containers
- Food ingredients in middle of preparation
- Gates
- Homework
- Old newspapers
- Stairs
- Trash
- Video game controllers
- Windows

These objects can normally go in inventory, but not if they're turned on:

- Alarm clock
- Dishwasher
- Phones
- Stereos
- Stoves
- Toaster oven
- TVs

Any custom-created artwork (from an easel) or photos (from photo booth or camera career object) can also be placed in inventory.

Love or hate letters from previous dates, once removed from the mailbox, also deposit in your Sim's inventory.

Sims' inventories are not useable on Community Lots. Though you can view the inventory while on a Community Lot, you won't be able to place or take objects (except for graves moved as described above).

Certain items are "carried" by your Sims but don't actually appear in your Sim's inventory. These include groceries and purchased video games and clothing. These are still automatically "installed" where they belong on your Sim's return home (in the fridge, all computers/game consoles, and dressers, respectively).

The exception to this rule is magazines. Though they previously functioned like other purchased items, they are now inventory items that you can place anywhere at home.

**note**

Players of the *University* expansion pack may notice the disappearance of the Give Handheld social. Since you can now remove the handheld game from your Sim's inventory and place it on the ground (where a child can claim it), the social is no longer necessary. If you don't have *University* and don't know what we're talking about...nothing to see here.

**tip**

Normally, when you move a family out of a lot, all of their possessions are liquidated and converted into cash. If you'd like to take your Sims' stuff with you to a new lot, pile it all into their inventory *before* moving them out. This is the only way to preserve career and Aspiration rewards, personal photos, and art, so be sure to pack those before moving.

If a Sim dies, anything in her inventory goes with her. You can, of course, regain access to these items by resurrecting your Sim with the Resurrect-O-Nomitron (from the *University* expansion pack).

# Changes to Create-A-Sim

The Create-A-Sim tool remains largely unchanged but includes a few new options to prepare your new Sims for the dating world.

You can choose the new Pleasure Aspiration right from the get-go in Create-A-Sim.

Panel 6 of Create-A-Sim boasts several new features:

Newly minted Sims must choose their Turn Ons and Turn Off in Create-A-Sim.

◆ The new Pleasure Aspiration can be selected just like original Aspirations.

◆ A new tab allows you to select your Sim's two Turn Ons and one Turn Off. You can't complete your Sim until both Aspiration and Turn Ons/Turn Off are set.

## Chapter 3

# New Aspirations

Aspirations give Sims' lives meaning and direction; something on which to focus all their energies over the span of years. *The Sims 2 Nightlife* introduces the first new Aspirations: Pleasure and Grilled Cheese (yes, you read that right).

This chapter outlines the specifics of these two new Aspirations and looks in detail at a new Aspiration reward object that empowers your Sims to change their Aspirations at will.

## Pleasure

Pleasure Sims love to be out on the town, dining, dating, bowling, or playing.

◆ Preferred Careers: Slacker, Politics, Artist, Culinary

◆ Skill Bent: Charisma, Creativity

◆ Sample Wants: Dine Out with Sim, Bowl with Sim, Have Dream Date, Have Great Outing, Be the DJ

◆ Sample Fears: Have Horrible Date, Be Rejected for Outing, Be Rejected for Dining with Sim

◆ Desperation Behavior: Mr. Party Guy

### Lifetime Wants:

◆ Go on 100 1st Dates

◆ Become Professional Party Guest (Slacker career)

◆ Have 50 Dream Dates

The Pleasure Aspiration is all about fun, but not necessarily the kind of things that feed the Fun need. It overlaps slightly and superficially resembles two existing Aspirations: Romance and Popularity. Like Romance Sims, Pleasure Sims hunger for amorous activity but not as exclusively. Like Popularity Sims, they desire a wide social network but not in just any form.

What Pleasure Sims really crave is the kinds of things downtown offers (even if those things are located at home or in their base neighborhood or college): dates, outings, fast cars, slow dancing, doing the smustle, bowling, manning the DJ booth, dining out, singing karaoke, meeting vampires, etc.

Date score is extremely important for Pleasure Sims because a bad date can realize some pretty powerful Fears.

Not surprisingly, most of their Fears revolve around having bad dates and outings, having their fun socials rejected, and embarrassing themselves in public (e.g., getting booed).

Good matches for Pleasure Sims are Fortune and other Pleasure Sims. Fortune Sims want to buy the kind of things that Pleasure Sims yearn to use, and they get satisfaction from going to work and making money, a commodity that fuels Pleasure Sims' pursuits. A pair of Pleasure Sims can be effective because it's easier to fulfill their Wants as a team. Because, however, money will have to come from somewhere, one of the Pleasure Sims will have to go to work and put aside his or her Wants.

Knowledge Sims are a bad match for Pleasure Sims because having fun and working are not major concerns and get in the way of their desires. A Knowledge Sim's home will likely be short on the kind of objects Pleasure Sims need to keep up their Aspiration score. Satisfying both Sims in such a relationship will be difficult because their Wants will at least indirectly conflict.

That's gonna leave a mark...a grill mark, that is.

# Grilled Cheese

- ◆ Preferred Careers: Culinary
- ◆ Skill Bent: Cooking
- ◆ Sample Wants: Eat Grilled Cheese, Serve Grilled Cheese, Make Grilled Cheese for Sim, Influence to Serve Grilled Cheese, Talk About Grilled Cheese
- ◆ Sample Fears: Be Rejected for Talk about Grilled Cheese, Burn Grilled Cheese, Eat Burned/Rotten/Spoiled Grilled Cheese
- ◆ Desperation Behavior: Mr. Grilled Cheese

## Lifetime Wants:

- ◆ Eat 200 Grilled Cheese Sandwiches

If you use the ReNuYuSenso Orb Aspiration reward object with green or lower Aspiration score, there's a risk that the object will fail and leave you with the socially awkward and nutritionally dicey Grilled Cheese Aspiration.

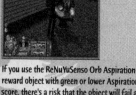

Grilled Cheese Sim making grilled cheese: happy Sim.

A Grilled Cheese Aspiration Sim derives Aspirational satisfaction from eating, cooking, talking about, and influencing others to make and eat grilled cheese. Clearly, keeping such a Sim content is a matter of ensuring a constant supply of grilled cheese-related stimulation rather than the more complicated demands

of the other Aspirations. Their sole Lifetime Want, for instance, is eating a whopping 200 grilled cheese sandwiches over a lifetime. This is a strategically simple but logistically challenging matter—making and eating this many grilled cheese sandwiches takes time and most of this Aspiration's wants are low-scoring.

Grilled Cheese Sim unable to make grilled cheese: unhappy Sim.

**tip**

A satisfied Grilled Cheese Sim will likely have difficulty keeping fit. Either be prepared to accept their constantly pudgy state or build in lots of time to exercise.

So inspired by the lowly grilled cheese sandwich are the Grilled Cheese Sims that they can prepare it regardless of Cooking skill (it normally requires Cooking 2) or time of day (mmm…grilled cheese for breakfast).

**tip**

Of course Cooking skill does still matter for the chance of burning your Sim's beloved grilled cheese. Because ruined sandwiches are a frequent Fear for these Sims, it behooves them to gain enough skill that scorching their grilled cheese is an infrequent occurrence. To make grilled cheese preparation nearly (95 percent) foolproof, develop Cooking skill to 4.

Though they don't need skill or observance of the clock, Sims can't cook grilled cheese without the necessary equipment:

◆ Refrigerator
◆ Stove
◆ At least one open countertop

If the Sim's lot lacks any of these essential tools, she'll display Wants to purchase these items and throw tantrums when her attempts to make grilled cheese are foiled for lack of the proper facilities.

**note**

If your Sim's new Grilled Cheese Aspiration doesn't appeal to you, get her Aspiration score up to Gold level (to ensure success), re-use the ReNuYuSenso Orb, and pick a less lunch-fare-oriented Aspiration.

If you're giving your Grilled Cheese Sim what he or she wants, these memories are going to pile up.

Every time Grilled Cheese Sims devour a grilled cheese sandwich, they receive a happy memory marker for what must be a spiritually fulfilling experience. Thereafter, they will talk, think, and dream about these memories.

Talk…About Grilled Cheese will be an unappealing topic for any but other Grilled Cheese Sims and very Nice Sims.

Finally, Grilled Cheese Sims get a special social: Talk …About Grilled Cheese. The Sims most likely to accept this somewhat stupefying topic of conversation are other Grilled Cheese Sims or, failing that, Nice ones. If the receiving Sim has less than five points in Grouchy/Nice and has any Aspiration besides Grilled Cheese, get ready for rejection.

Grilled Cheese Sims are really only fit company for other Grilled Cheese Sims, but they don't substantially interfere with the Wants of any other Aspiration.

# Aspiration Monikers

## Teen Monikers by Aspiration

| Aspiration Level | Pleasure | Grilled Cheese |
|---|---|---|
| Distress—Moderate to Severe | Delightless Downer | Wayward Wenslydale Whelp |
| Distress—Low to Moderate | Bummed-out Bore | Frustrated Feta Fondler |
| Green—Low | Callow Contentment Craver | Jarlsburg Using Youth |
| Green—High | Freshfaced Funlover | Precocious Parmesan Preparer |
| Gold | Junior Joy Jockey | Cheshire-Chomping Champion |
| Platinum | Euphoric Youth | Juvenile Jack Genius |

## Adult/Young Adult Monikers by Aspiration

| Aspiration Level | Pleasure | Grilled Cheese |
|---|---|---|
| Distress—Moderate to Severe | Narcissistic Knucklehead | Bumbling Brie Burner |
| Distress—Low to Moderate | Downfaced Drag | Chedder-lacking Chucklehead |
| Green—Low | Common Comfortlover | Common Camembert Coveter |
| Green—High | Hearty Hedonist | Gouda Gobbling Gourmet |
| Gold | Frolicking Freespirit | Exceptional Edam Eater |
| Platinum | Primo/Prima Pleasureseeker | Muenster Munching Maniac |

## Elder Monikers by Aspiration

| Aspiration Level | Pleasure | Grilled Cheese |
|---|---|---|
| Distress—Moderate to Severe | Grave-faced Grumbler | Run-down Roquefort Ruiner |
| Distress—Low to Moderate | Dried-up Discontent | Mature Mozzarella Mangler |
| Green—Low | Satisfied Silvermane | Grill Greasin' Granny/Grandpa |
| Green—High | Fossilized Funmeister | Excellent Emmental Elder |
| Gold | Gray-haired Glee-grabber | Legendary Limburger Lover |
| Platinum | Long-lived Levity-liker | Senior Stilton Sorcerer |

# New Aspiration Reward Object

Reward objects empower your Sims to do many things or make big, otherwise unavailable changes to their lives. Until now, however, nothing except a college education permitted your Sims to change

eir Aspirations; once chosen, they were pretty
uch set for life. Likewise, your Sims' new Turn
ff and Turn Ons are not easily changed for
ewly created Sims.

If, however, your Sim is reasonably successful
n her current Aspiration (enough to amass some
spiration points and, ideally, get her Aspiration
to gold or platinum range), she can use a new
eward object to switch her life to a new track or
hange her Turn Ons or Turn Off.

### note

The First time you load
the *The Sims 2
Nightlife* expansion
ack, all of your existing teen
d older Sims are randomly
assigned their Turn Ons and
urn Off. Since this is a
ecessary but not
ntirely fair step, they
so get a ReNuYu
orta-Chug potion
highlighted by the
ypsy Matchmaker the first time
ou load a preexisting lot]
eposited in their inventory.
rinking this potion has the
ame effect as the
eNuYuSenso Orb, allowing you a
ree chance to change the
im's Turn Ons and Turn Off
though not Aspiration].

Once it's been imbibed,
here's no way to get a new
ial of this potion; all future
hanges must be made with
he Orb. Unless, of course,
ne of your other playable
lims can part with her
otion. To transfer a potion,
lace it on the ground from
he giving Sim's inventory,
witch to the receiving Sim,
nd drag it into his inventory.

Preexisting Sims get a ReNuYu Porta-Chug potion in their inventory
that enacts some of the same changes as the ReNuYuSenso Orb.

As with all reward objects, however, using this
object with green or red Aspiration level could
result in untoward consequences (mmmm...
grilled cheese).

## ReNuYuSenso Orb

- ◆ Used by: Teen/Adult/Young Adult/Elder
- ◆ Reward Point Cost: 6,250
- ◆ Uses/Time Limit: 5
- ◆ Success: Sim has opportunity to change Aspiration, Turn Ons,
  and/or Turn Off.
- ◆ Failure: Sim emerges with the Grilled Cheese Aspiration and the
  immediate urge to make a sandwich.

Use the ReNuYuSenso
Orb and reprogram your
Sim's Aspiration and
Turn Ons/Turn Off.

### caution

Note that changing an Aspiration will give
your Sim a new Lifetime Want. If you later
change back to your original Aspiration,
you may not receive the same Lifetime Want your Sim
had before. Changing Turn Ons or Turn Offs, however,
will have no effect on Lifetime Want.

# The Sims 2 Nightlife EXPANSION PACK

## Chapter 4

# ATTRACTION AND CHEMISTRY

Attraction and Chemistry measure how naturally suited to one another two Sims are. They also serve as a very potent relationship accelerator. If Attraction and Chemistry exist, high-level relationships can be built much more quickly. Attraction and Chemistry are not, therefore, a requirement for romance, but having strong Chemistry sure does make it easier. Likewise, folks who are different enough to actually repel each other will have the most difficult time getting together: hard but not impossible.

This chapter will help you understand the intricacies of Attraction and Chemistry and enable you to harness this new system to turbocharge your relationships and dating exploits. Romance and Pleasure Sims especially better fasten their seat belts!

## Attraction

Your Sim rates every other Sim whom he or she meets (with some exceptions) by how attractive they are. Likewise, every other Sim is evaluating your Sim for his or her attractiveness. A Sim's attractiveness is not inherent, but is in the eye of the beholder. A Sim who's very attractive to one of your Sims may be repellant to another. Attraction, as you'll see, depends on many relative factors (personality, Aspiration, and Turn Offs and Turn Ons to name a few).

Attraction doesn't necessarily go both ways.

**note**
Unlike Chemistry, Attraction is not ruled by gender preference. In what circumstances Attraction comes into play, however, is. For some purposes, Sims' Attraction to a Sim of their non-preferred gender may be important and they'll display it if they do the Check Sim Out interaction. In other circumstances, however, only the attractiveness of Sims of your Sim's preferred gender will be considered.

Attraction to another Sim is not only relative but also unilateral. In other words, there's no guarantee that a Sim your Sim finds attractive will think the same of him or her. In fact, the same variable that makes the other Sim so luscious to your Sim may be the exact factor that makes your Sim a major dud to him or her.

**note**
There are two classes of Sims that your Sim will not even consider for Attraction (1) Sims to whom your Sim is related by blood and (2) Sims who are age-inappropriate. Children are not attractive to any other Sim and teens are attractive only to other teens. Young adults, adults, and elders, however, are free to find each other attractive regardless of age.

Thus, it's important to understand that Attraction is not necessarily mutual and high Attraction from your Sim is no guarantee of the other Sim's feelings in response.

# ATTRACTION AND CHEMISTRY

**note**

You can, as you'll see, inquire about another Sim's Attraction to your Sim and, in some cases, even change your Sim to make him or her more attractive to that Sim.

Hubba-hubba! We guess we know who's attractive to whom.

### What impact does attractiveness have:

1. It contributes to the "Chemistry" between two Sims (see below). Chemistry is the mechanism that makes relationship building easier or harder based on a couple's average Attraction to each other.

2. Attraction affects a Sim's autonomous behavior. When Sims are near a Sim they find attractive, they'll make no secret of it, gesturing and expressing their admiration.

3. Attraction is a requirement of some socials. These socials don't require any specific level of Attraction, but they do require that the other Sim be eligible for Attraction. In other words, socials that require Attraction can only be performed on Sims of the appropriate age who are not blood relations.

4. A Sim's Attraction level to the date or loved one of another Sim can trigger in them romantic rivalry behavior. For more info, see Chapter 9.

5. Attraction contributes to the starting score of dates: the higher the Attraction, the more of a head start the date receives.

6. Attraction causes Sims, even Sims with whom your Sim has not yet interacted, to appear in their thoughts.

7. Another Sim's Attraction to your Sim dictates the Sim's response to the Ask...Do You Like What You See? social.

8. Your Sim's Attraction to another Sim dictates your Sim's response to the Flirt...Check Sim Out social.

9. Your Sim's Attraction to every Sim in a room dictates the response to the Scope Room self-interaction.

## Attraction and Gender Preference

**note**

In general, gender preference dictates how Sims behave autonomously (when they're deciding on their own what actions to take). A female-gender preference Sim will, therefore, never autonomously choose to do a Flirt with a male Sim. This doesn't mean Sims will refuse if *directed* to Flirt with a male; they just won't do it on their own.

First, however, a note on gender preference. Every Sim (except ones fresh out of Create-A-Sim) has a gender preference that's defined by the sum total of all his or her romantic interactions. If most of these interactions have been with male Sims, your Sim has a preference for males. If most have been with females, your Sim's gender preference is female. If your Sim prefers women but does enough romantic interactions with men over time, the preference will eventually change as the balance shifts.

This Sim can't scope the room because she has no gender preference.

This is important because your Sim will only autonomously act out Attraction to Sims of their preferred gender. Any Sims of the other gender won't register, for example, in the Scope Room interaction. In fact, a Sim who has established no gender preference won't be able to do the Scope Room interaction.

**tip**

To quickly set gender preference. Find a Sim of the desired gender and do a low-level Flirt interaction (e.g., Wolf Whistle or Check Sim Out). There: gender preference set.

# Elements of Attraction

Whether a Sim ("Sim A") is attracted to another Sim ("Sim B") is a function of six factors:

- Personality similarities
- A and B's Aspirations
- A's Turn Ons
- B's zodiac sign
- A and B's preexisting relationships
- A's Turn Off

Each factor accounts for a portion of A's total Attraction to Sim B (or B's attractiveness to A). How much of each of those portions are awarded, however, depend on the specifics.

**note**

To give you a sense of scale in the rare moments when we bandy about attractiveness numbers, it's helpful to understand the scale of the invisible Attraction score. A Sim's Attraction to another Sim can range from a maximum of 150 to a minimum of -140. Thus, something that alters Attraction by 50 points, for example, is pretty significant.

## Personality Similarities

These Sims have very similar personalities and could be quite attracted to each other if everything else falls into place.

The more closely two Sims' personalities match, the more attracted they'll be to each other. To determine *how intensely* attractive a Sim is to another Sim, each personality factor is compared and the differences in each factor are added together. The resulting score measures how "similar" their personalities are.

**note**

Perfectly matching personalities can boost Chemistry by one level.

Thus Sims with identical personalities receive the maximum personality similarity score. Likewise, two Sims with diametrically opposed scores in every personality factor get the lowest possible similarities score. Everyone else will be somewhere in between.

**note**

Because this factor is the same for both Sims, it contributes the same amount to each Sim's Attraction scores.

An example:

| Personality Trait | Sim A | Sim B | Difference |
|---|---|---|---|
| Neat/Sloppy | 4 | 4 | 0 |
| Outgoing/Shy | 4 | 7 | 3 |
| Active/Lazy | 4 | 6 | 2 |
| Playful/Serious | 7 | 3 | 4 |
| Nice/Grouchy | 6 | 5 | 1 |
| TOTAL: | — | — | 10 |

Identical personalities would give a total difference of 0 while completely opposed personalities would yield a difference of 50. A difference of 0 points, therefore, would get the *highest* score for personality similarity (*more attractive*) and a comparison of 50 would get *no* score for personality similarity (*less attractive*). Thus, in our example above, a difference of 10 gets this couple pretty high Attraction as to their personalities.

### note

Though you can't create a Sim with either 0 or 10 in every personality trait, such extreme personalities are possible. There are ways in the game to forge these extremities, so it's not impossible.

Ask about a Sim's zodiac sign to find out his or her personality.

There's no way to inquire about a non-playable Sim's personality directly, but you can get a general idea by using the Ask...What's Your Sign social.

Because zodiac signs are actually general personality profiles, knowing a Sim's sign gives you a ballpark guess at his or her personality traits. For example, a Libra will (as shown in the table below) be (give or take a digit or two):

◆ Neat/Sloppy: 2
◆ Outgoing/Shy: 8
◆ Active/Lazy: 2
◆ Playful/Serious: 6
◆ Nice/Grouchy: 7

Without doing a detailed calculation, you can quickly gauge how big a difference there is and whether it'll significantly reduce another Sim's attractiveness or the attractiveness of your Sim to the other.

### Personality Presets by Zodiac Sign

| Zodiac Sign | Neat | Outgoing | Active | Playful | Nice |
|---|---|---|---|---|---|
| Aries | 5 | 8 | 6 | 3 | 3 |
| Taurus | 5 | 5 | 3 | 8 | 4 |
| Gemini | 4 | 7 | 8 | 3 | 3 |
| Cancer | 6 | 3 | 6 | 4 | 6 |
| Leo | 4 | 10 | 4 | 4 | 3 |
| Virgo | 9 | 2 | 6 | 3 | 5 |
| Libra | 2 | 8 | 2 | 6 | 7 |
| Scorpio | 6 | 5 | 8 | 3 | 3 |
| Sagittarius | 2 | 3 | 9 | 7 | 4 |
| Capricorn | 7 | 4 | 1 | 8 | 5 |
| Aquarius | 4 | 4 | 4 | 7 | 6 |
| Pisces | 5 | 3 | 7 | 3 | 7 |

## Zodiac

Beyond what it reveals about your Sim's personality, a Sim's zodiac sign independently contributes to his or her attractiveness.

Every zodiac sign has two signs to which it's attracted and from which it's repelled. All other signs are neutral.

In determining Attraction, therefore, Sims with your Sim's favored signs get a boost in attractiveness and Sims with your Sim's disfavored signs see a reduction. Likewise, your Sim will be extra attractive if his or her sign is one of the two that appeals to the other Sim or less attractive if it's one of the bad ones. If a sign is neither attractive nor repellant, it has no effect on attractiveness.

## Zodiac Sign Compatibility

| Zodiac Sign | Attracted to | Repelled by |
|---|---|---|
| Aries | Gemini/Taurus | Cancer/Libra |
| Taurus | Aries/Libra | Virgo/Cancer |
| Gemini | Pisces/Virgo | Capricorn/Aries |
| Cancer | Taurus/Scorpio | Gemini/Aries |
| Leo | Sagittarius/Cancer | Capricorn/Gemini |
| Virgo | Aquarius/Sagittarius | Leo/Taurus |
| Libra | Virgo/Cancer | Pisces/Scorpio |
| Scorpio | Pisces/Leo | Libra/Aquarius |
| Sagittarius | Pisces/Capricorn | Libra/Scorpio |
| Capricorn | Aquarius/Taurus | Leo/Gemini |
| Aquarius | Capricorn/Sagittarius | Scorpio/Virgo |
| Pisces | Scorpio/Gemini | Leo/Aries |

**note**

Using both personality differences and zodiac to determine attractiveness may seem redundant, but it does provide one important distinction. Personality difference dictates that the most attractive personality is one that's identical. However, identical personalities always have the same zodiac sign. Because no sign favors itself in the table above, the points gained from being a favored sign will never be available.

Thus, in terms of these two factors, a Sim with minor personality differences and a favored zodiac sign will be more attractive than an identical personality Sim.

## Aspirations

Sims care about personality but they also care about a Sim's goals and vision. That's why a Sim's Aspiration can add to or reduce attractiveness.

**note**

How important are complementary Aspirations? Having them bumps up two Sims' Chemistry by a whole level. Conversely, a negative Aspiration match drops Chemistry by a level.

When on a date, the other Sim's Aspiration is shown on the Date Score Meter.

The table below shows what effect every combination of Aspirations has on the Attraction between two Sims. A combination can add to attractiveness ("+"), reduce attractiveness ("-"), or have no effect ("Neutral"). In one case, the correct combination actually adds *substantially* to Attraction.

## Aspiration and Attraction

| Aspiration | Romance | Wealth | Popularity | Family | Knowledge | Pleasure | Grilled Cheese |
|---|---|---|---|---|---|---|---|
| Romance | + | Neutral | + | - | - | Neutral | Neutral |
| Wealth | Neutral | + | - | + | Neutral | + | + |
| Popularity | Neutral | - | + | Neutral | - | - | Neutral |
| Family | - | Neutral | Neutral | + | + | - | Neutral |
| Knowledge | - | - | Neutral | Neutral | + | Neutral | Neutral |
| Pleasure | + | + | Neutral | - | Neutral | + | + |
| Grilled Cheese | Neutral | Neutral | Neutral | Neutral | Neutral | Neutral | + |

**note**

All Sims are attracted to Sims with the same Aspirations (Grilled Cheese exclusively so). Note, however, that most other positive combinations aren't mutual. For example, Romance Sims favor Popularity Sims, but Popularity Sims are neutral toward Romance Sims. Peruse the table and look for mutual combinations for optimal two-way attractiveness.

**note**

On top of the Aspiration bonus, Grilled Cheese Sims get an extra bonus (+75 points) in Chemistry with other Grilled Cheese Sims. For example, if two Sims with repellant Chemistry both become Grilled Cheese Sims, their chemistry rises to around medium.

## Preexisting Relationships

Sometimes Attraction comes after a relationship has already begun to blossom. That's why various preexisting relationships (e.g., marriage, love, etc.) independently contribute to a Sim's attractiveness.

Two Sims who've already earned their relationship stripes doesn't need Chemistry or Attraction.

These relationships enhance attractiveness not by adding to it, but by providing a minimum below which, as long as the relationship type exists, Attraction can never drop. Thus, if two Sims with no actual Attraction fall in love and get married, their effective attractiveness to each other increases merely because they're married.

If two Sims share any of the following relationships, Attraction will never be below neutral except for the existence of a Turn Off:

- ◆ Married
- ◆ Engaged
- ◆ Steady
- ◆ Love
- ◆ Crush
- ◆ Lifetime Relationship greater than 70

## Turn Ons and Turn Offs

Most of the factors discussed thus far are largely unchangeable elements of your Sim that aren't worth altering just for the sake of increasing Attraction. Thus, they don't have much strategic value; either the factors align or they don't.

Your Sims' Turn Ons and Turn Offs can be viewed in their Simology panel, under Chemistry.

That's why every Sim has two Turn Ons and one Turn Off. If another Sim possesses one of these features, it can dramatically shift his or her attractiveness (negatively for Turn Offs and positively for Turn Ons). Just a single matching Turn On can raise Chemistry by one level and maximum Attraction will be impossible without at least one Turn On match.

Sims created with The Sims 2 Nightlife installed must have their Turn Ons/Offs set at inception.

Turn Offs, on the other hand, are even more powerful. A single Turn Off can neutralize two Turn Ons. To put it another way, it can lower Chemistry by two levels.

Sims can be turned on or off by any of the following characteristics:

- Black Hair
- Blonde Hair
- Brown Hair
- Cologne
- Custom Hair
- Facial Hair
- Fatness
- Fitness
- Formalwear
- Full Face Makeup
- Glasses
- Grey Hair
- Hats
- Makeup
- Red Hair
- Stink
- Swimwear
- Underwear
- Vampirism

**note**

Existing Sims have their Turn Ons and Turn Offs set automatically, though there are some restrictions. For example, a male Sim with a female gender preference won't be randomly assigned facial hair as a Turn On or Turn Off because it's not possible.

What all these things have in common is that they are easily changeable. If you want your Sim to be attractive to a specific Sim, you can find out what their Turn Offs and Turn Ons are and endeavor to match them.

How each factors is changed, however, varies. See "Turn On and Turn Off Strategy," below.

**tip**

When you're out on the town, keep a bottle of cologne in your inventory, just in case that special someone prefers your Sim to be wearing it.

## Discovering Turn Ons and Turn Offs

Never hurts to ask. Find out what a Sim's Turn Offs and Turn Ons are and you can change your Sim to fit.

As with most elements of Attraction, the easiest way is to just ask. By using Ask...What Turns You On and Ask...What Turns You Off, you'll get the straight answer. Note that you may have to ask several times to learn both Turn Ons because which one the Sim reveals is chosen at random.

"Eww, I hate your black hair!" A Sim reveals the reason for her repulsion; she's turned off by black hair.

The other way to discover Turn Ons and Turn Offs is to use the Ask...Do You Like What You See? social. In response to this question, Sims reveal whether they find your Sim attractive and the primary reason why. If their Attraction to your Sim is due to the presence or absence of a Turn On or if the lack of Attraction is due to a Turn Off, they'll display the appropriate Turn On/Off in their response. With this information, you can (if you wish) make a change to your Sim to fit that Turn On or eliminate a Turn Off.

**note**

For more info on the Ask socials in general and the Ask...Do You Like What You See? social in particular, see Chapter 7.

## Turn On and Turn Off Strategy

Turn Ons and Turn Offs are major factors in Attraction. Though two Sims can be quite attracted to each other with no Turn Ons, they can't reach the highest levels without at least one per Sim. Likewise, an otherwise incompatible couple can find each other positively scintillating if they play into each other's Turn Ons. On the other hand, sporting a Sim's Turn Off is a guaranteed Attraction killer.

A little look in the mirror may be all it takes to make your Sim considerably more attractive.

Fortunately, Turn Ons and Turn Offs are, generally, under your control:

◆ Hair color, facial hair, hats, glasses, makeup, and full face makeup can be changed in any mirror with the Change Appearance interaction.

◆ Vampirism can be acquired by being bitten by a vampire, or undone (if your Sim's intended considers the undead a turn *off*) by drinking Vamprocillin-D potion. See Chapter 10.

◆ Change into or out of underwear, swimwear, and formalwear with a visit to your home dresser.

◆ Fatness or fitness can be changed by working out (to gain fitness) or overeating (to get fatter).

◆ Cologne can be acquired from cologne displays on Community Lots. To count for a Turn On or Off, however, the cologne must be sprayed on, not just held in inventory. Cologne can be removed by taking a shower, a bath, a swim, or a sponge bath.

◆ Stink can be removed by bathing and can be acquired by letting Hygiene drop until the telltale green cloud forms.

**note**
One other thing that can affect attractiveness is the Gypsy Matchmaker's Love Potion #8.5. This attractiveness enhancer is discussed in "Love Potion #8.5," later in this chapter.

## Changing Your Sims' Turn Ons and Turn Offs

Until now, we've discussed Turn On/Off strategy in terms of altering your Sims' characteristics to make them more attractive to another particular Sim. You can, however, take the opposite approach and change your Sim's Turn On and Turn Offs to match the attributes of the desired Sim. There are several ways to do this:

To consume the Porta-Chug, just click on your Sim.

◆ ReNuYu Porta-Chug: Every Sim in your game when you installed the *The Sims 2 Nightlife* expansion was randomly assigned their Turn Ons/Offs. Each of them has one free opportunity to change these by consuming the potion. This potion can be given to any other Sim, even one created *after* you installed the expansion pack, by removing it from your Sim's inventory and leaving it on the ground on a home lot. From there, you can direct another playable Sim to pick it up and, once it's in inventory, drink it.

◆ ReNuYuSenso Orb: Spend your Sims' Aspiration points for a five-use Aspiration reward that allows changing of both Aspiration and/or Turn Ons and Turn Offs. You can make this change as many times as you can afford it, but use it only with Gold or better Aspiration score or the process might fail.

Using the ReNuYuSenso Orb with low Aspiration score could lead to unintended consequences.

# Seeing Attraction in Action

You have several tools to discover both which Sims your Sim finds attractive and how attractive other Sims find your Sim to be.

## Scope Room (Self-Interaction)

Scope the room to discover who your Sim finds the hottest.

The Scope Room interaction is available when you click on your own Sim. The Sim scans the room he or she's currently in and highlights which Sim or Sims, if any, he or she finds most attractive. If no Sims meet a minimum standard of attractiveness, your Sim simply shrugs and moves on.

If, however, attractive Sims are present, the most attractive Sims briefly glow white and a note informs you which of them are the most attractive.

Keep in mind, this is not a reflection of how attractive the other Sim will find your Sim nor of both Sims' collective Chemistry. It's merely who your Sim finds most attractive. To discover Chemistry, you'll have make your Sim meet the other Sim.

## Flirt...Check Sim Out

Check Sim Out is a Flirt interaction that works like a one-on-one Scope Room. Choose a Sim (even if the Sim is not of your Sim's preferred gender) and select Check Sim Out to see if your Sim finds that particular Sim attractive.

**note**
A Sim fresh out of Create-A-Sim will have no gender preference and, thus, won't express Attraction, display Chemistry, or be able to do the Scope Room interaction. Not, that is, until the Sim does at least one romantic interaction that sets gender preference. Because Check Sim Out is always accepted and has no relationship effects, it's a risk-free way to quickly define which way your Sim is oriented.

This Sim is juuuust right.

If the other Sim is to your Sim's liking, he or she will display a shower of small pink and red hearts around an image of the Sim.

# ATTRACTION AND CHEMISTRY

Not so much. Oh well.

If your Sim is unmoved by the chosen Sim, he or she will display a picture of the Sim and shrug.

Gag me with a reticulated spline!! You ain't my cup of tea!

If your Sim finds the other Sim *unattractive*, he or she displays a shower of red "X"'s around an image of the Sim.

## Ask...Do You Like What You See?

This interaction determines whether the other Sim finds your Sim attractive and why. He or she can respond in one of several ways:

### note
If the reaction to this social is not because of a Turn On or Off, it's because of one of the other factors or a combination.

Attracted because of Turn On: Shows thought balloon of Turn On and hubba-hubba gesture.

Attracted to but no Turn Ons: Shows thought balloon of your Sim with a shower of hearts.

Neutral despite both Turn Ons: Shows thought balloon of your Sim with an "X."

Neutral because of lack of a Turn On: Shrug and shows thought balloon with a Turn On. This serves as a suggestion for something your Sim could change to become more attractive.

Neutral because of a Turn Off: Shows red "X" thought balloon of Turn Off.

Not attracted: Shows red "X" hearts and thought balloon of your Sim.

Not attracted because of Turn Off. Shows red "X" thought balloon of Turn Off.

Examine Sims' Relationship panels to find their Chemistry levels with every Sim they know.

Unlike Attraction, Chemistry is visible in-game, appearing as a symbol in the Relationship panel. If both Sims prefer each other's gender, the first time two Sims meet (with any kind of interaction), the other Sim will be added each Sim's Relationship panel with identical lightning-bolt-shaped symbols, representing Chemistry. Each version of the symbol represents one of the five levels of Chemistry:

The Chemistry sort in the Relationship panel shows only Sims with whom your Sim has mild or better Chemistry.

## tip

Any updates to Attraction cause a Sim's Wants/Fears panel to refresh. This can be desirable because Wants can become stale if not invalid if not refreshed for a while. During a date, especially, it's helpful to see your Sim's date's Wants as up-to-date as possible, so periodically do a Do You Like What You See? to force both Sim's Wants to update.

- ◆  Three Lightning Bolts: Strong (average Attraction 70–150)
- ◆ Two Lightning Bolts: Medium (average Attraction 36–70)
- ◆ One Lightning Bolt: Mild (average Attraction 11–35)
- ◆ No Icon: Neutral (average Attraction -10–10)
- ◆ One Lightning Bolt with Red "X": Repulsion (average Attraction -140–-10)

# Chemistry

The average of two Sims' Attraction to each other is called "Chemistry."

## note

Your Sims have Chemistry only with Sims of their preferred gender. If gender preference changes, however, Chemistry will be shown in your Sim's Relationship panel for all Sims of the newly preferred gender and the icons will be removed from all Sims of the formerly preferred gender.

A Chemistry rating, unlike Attraction, is mutual between two Sims, reflecting an average of each Sim's independent Attraction to the other. Thus if Sim A is strongly attracted to Sim B but Sim B is only mildly attracted to Sim A, each will display a Chemistry score of Medium (two lightning bolts).

# ATTRACTION AND CHEMISTRY

## Chemistry and Social Interactions

The Chemistry between two Sims can, if high enough, alter the social interactions between them, making available interactions requiring higher relationships and lowering the relationship requirements for accepting social interactions. Thus, two Sims who don't know each other well enough to kiss romantically by normal standards can try the interaction and have it accepted if they have sufficient Chemistry. The result: faster relationship building.

## Chemistry and Interaction Availability

Interactions available solely because of Chemistry are highlighted with a lightning-bolt icon.

Whether an interaction appears on your Sim's interaction menu is a matter of availability. Interactions become available when your Sim meets the interactions availability requirements. For example, Kiss...Peck requires your Sim have a Daily Relationship of 40–100 and a Lifetime Relationship of 20–100 with Sim B before it'll even appear on the menu.

Chemistry lowers the relationship requirements for all interactions to appear on the menu. The higher the Chemistry, the lower the requirements will go.

Additionally, high Chemistry removes the Crush and Love requirements from some interactions (e.g., Make Out), making them available when no crush or love relationship exists.

Interactions available *solely* because of Chemistry sport a lightning bolt icon.

**note**

When your Sim surpasses an interaction's normal availability requirement, the lightning bolt icon disappears because Chemistry is no longer the reason it's available.

Thus, your Sim can attempt higher-level interactions earlier in a relationship.

Of course, whether an interaction appears on the menu has *nothing* to do with whether it'll be accepted—that depends on factors belonging to the interaction's recipient. This is, as you know, called "acceptance."

## Chemistry and Interaction Acceptance

Acceptance is the basis on which the target of an interaction accepts or rejects the interaction based on his or her relationship toward the other Sim. Often, acceptance can also depend on other factors including the target Sim's personality, skills, etc.

Chemistry aside, the availability of an interaction doesn't mean it'll work.

Chemistry also reduces the relationship requirements for accepting all interactions. Thus, a Sim with a relatively low relationship will accept a romantic interaction if Chemistry is high enough.

## note

For the availability and acceptance of interactions, two Sims with maximum Chemistry should be able to perform any interactions as successfully as two Sims who have just fallen in love.

Conversely, repellant Sims should have access to the same socials as two Sims who've repeatedly slapped each other.

The greater the Chemistry, the lower the relationship standards will fall and the earlier interactions will be accepted.

## tip

Chemistry brings down acceptance requirements quite a bit, but don't get too hasty. Aim too high with your romantic advances and you'll hurt the relationship more than you'll help it.

## note

When the Gypsy Matchmaker chooses someone for your Sim's blind date, the amount you pay determines what level of Chemistry the matchmaker will choose.

## Love Potion #8.5

There is one other way to boost your Sim's attractiveness and, thus, his or her Chemistry level with all other Sims, but it requires a bit of hocus pocus and some simoleans.

Love Potion #8.5 is purchased from the Gypsy Matchmaker and placed in your Sim's inventory. When consumed, it increases your Sim's attractiveness to all other Sims by 100 points for three hours.

## note

A 100-point rise in attractiveness means a 50-point increase in Chemistry or enough to raise Chemistry by at least one level.

Once he or she has consumed the potion, your Sim emits pink and red hearts wherever he or she wanders until the potion's effect wears off.

During this time, your Sim's Chemistry scores with all preferred gender Sims is much higher. Use the time productively by aggressively socializing to quickly build up relationships.

Be very careful not to drink a love potion while another is still at work. Doubling up potions can randomly cause a violent and unseemly reaction. The drinker will gag and his or her Hygiene and Comfort will drop to zero. What's more, any Sim's Attraction to the drinker will be lowered to rock-bottom until the potion wears off.

## Chapter 5

# GOING OUT: DATES, GROUPS, AND OUTINGS

Getting away from home has long been a favorite pastime of the average Sim. But, as any social butterfly knows, gathering a bunch of friends can be like herding cats. Plus, it's never easy to have a great date when your companion is wandering off to play pinball or grab a snack.

With *The Sims 2 Nightlife*, these precious social gatherings have a new shape, a new feel, and—most of all—a new system of scoring and rewards that make going out more than just having a few laughs.

This chapter examines the details, big and small, that are the difference between a dud of a date and fabulous foray.

**note**
One of the handiest benefits to the new dating/gathering system is that any properly assembled social group will stick together, use group objects together, dine as a unit, and move from lot to lot as a team. Pretty much the only place a date or gathering Sim won't follow your Sim is to the bathroom.

Individual Sims may break away from the group to tend to their needs but they will, generally, hang together and follow your Sim's lead.

## Dates

Dates are two-Sim gatherings that are timed and scored. When successful, dates build a relationship faster than standard socializing and provide several possible rewards. They're also lots of fun for the Sims involved.

**note**
A few simple rules apply for who can be dated. Obviously no Sim can date children or toddlers or non-spouse family members. Teens may only date teens. Adults, young adults, and elders may date any adult, young adult, or elder. Within those confines, go for it.

## How to Get a Date

Straight up asking is the most common, if not the most surefire, route to a date.

You can start a date in one of four ways:

1. **Call...Ask Out on Date:** Available on any house or cell phone. Only date-eligible Sims your Sim has met can be invited to a date by phone. Calling between midnight and 7 a.m. results in a hostile rejection and a reduction in Daily Relationship (the same as any other middle-of-the-night telephone call).

2. **Ask...On Date:** Asking in person, available on any date-eligible Sim.

3. **Be asked by another Sim** by phone. This only happens after one successful date with that Sim.

4. **Gypsy Matchmaker:** Summon the Gypsy Matchmaker via the telephone Services menu and, for a sliding fee, she sets up an immediate date with a randomly selected Sim. The Chemistry

level of the date depends on how much you spend. This is the easiest way to get a date because it can't be rejected.

Getting a date by phone is just like in person except it can be done with Sims who aren't on the lot.

The Gypsy Matchmaker can pull a date right out of the sky, if your Sim has the cash.

**note**

Asking someone for a date is considered a romantic social and therefore, will affect your Sim's gender preference and trigger jealousy in other Sims. If, therefore, your Sim asks for a date when a spouse, fiancé, steady, love, crush, or a date-in-progress is present, the other Sim reacts with jealousy. Of course, any spurned Sim will be furious at your Sim for quite some time (see Chapter 9).

Attraction-eligible Sims will either accept or reject the date offer based on:

**note**

Recall that "Attraction-eligible" means a Sim is of an appropriate age for Attraction to your Sim and a non-spousal family member. Gender preference does not impact who is Attraction-eligible, though it does dictate toward whom Sims will autonomously express their

attraction. In other words, Sims are aware of some level of Attraction to every Attraction-eligible Sim regardless of gender but only display their Attraction to their preferred gender.

Don't ask out just anyone for a date; if that Sim doesn't know your Sim at least a little, he or she will likely not-so-politely decline.

1. Mood
2. Daily Relationship
3. Lifetime Relationship
4. Outgoing or Nice personality

Generally speaking, if the asked Sim's Mood is positive and his Daily and Lifetime Relationship toward your Sim has been moderately developed (above 25 Daily and 10 Lifetime), he or she will agree to the date. If the relationship isn't that developed, a high Outgoing or high Nice Sim will still accept, but only if that Sim is in a solidly good Mood.

## Where to Date?

When making a date by phone, you have to decide where it'll take place.

The next step is to decide where the date will occur.

Dates can be either on a Community Lot or at home.

### tip

Your Sim can travel to a Community Lot date via either taxi or a personal car. Note that the *kind* of car you use to pick up a date can affect a Date score depending on the date's personality. For example, Outgoing Sims prefer to be picked up in the Hunka 711 whereas Serious Sims prefer the Yomoshoto Evasion. You get extra Date points for equipping your Sim with the right ride.

1. On a Community Lot (you can specify which one later): If the date is accepted, you have one hour to leave your Sim's lot. If you don't leave before that time, the date will be stood up (see below).

2. At your Sim's home. The invited Sim shows up soon after you hang up, so be ready for the date before you make the call. Your Sim automatically greets the date when he or she arrives.

### note

If you have the *The Sims 2 University* expansion pack installed, there's a dating limitation you must be aware of. Due to stuffy but ironclad rules of the secret society, dates can not be made on or brought to secret society lots.

### note

If you ask for a date in person, the date begins immediately wherever your Sims are. If you'd then like to move the date to a Community Lot, the date will follow your Sim on the trip.

### tip

For a home date, try to prepare food before you invite the date over. There's a risk the food will go to waste if your Sim is turned down, but it's better than wasting valuable date time cooking.

## Standing Up

If you don't leave to pick up a Community Lot date within one hour of the invitation, the date will decide that he or she has been stood up.

Once you set up a date, remember to get your Sim where he or she needs to be. Forget and face the consequences.

Standing up a date results in a reduction in both Daily and Lifetime Relationship, an angry phone call, and a moderate furious state.

## The Date Meter

The Date Meter tells you how the date is going but also so much more.

As soon as the date begins, the Date Meter appears in the screen's upper right. This thermometer-looking device tells you several things:

◆ How well the date is going (the "Date score")

◆ How much time is *currently* remaining (time can be added; see below)

◆ Whom the date is with

◆ The date's Aspiration icon

◆ The date's current Wants and Fears (click on the Aspiration icon)

The Date Meter is divided into seven sectors, each representing a quality of date:

◆ Dream Date ◆ Great
◆ Good ◆ Okay
◆ Lame ◆ Bad
◆ Horrible

The Date Level when time expires is the final score for the date. If Date score reaches rock bottom for any reason before the clock winds down, the "mercy rule" kicks in and the date ends immediately; there's no recovering from a date that awful. The dreamiest of Dream Dates, however, can go on until time runs out even if score is pegged at maximum.

**note**

During a date, your Sim's date is highlighted with a blue plumb bob. This plumb bob, unlike the one that adorns your active Sim, is smaller and doesn't change color to reflect the Sim's Mood. If the date is between two Sims from the same household—both, therefore, are playable—whichever Sim is not being played at a given moment will have the blue plumb bob. Switch and the previously controlled Sim gets the blue bob.

## Date Score

The Date score is a measure of how well the date is going. Points are added to or subtracted from the Date score based on events that occur during the date. If the Sims on the date share a hug, their score changes. If they dance the smustle together, it affects their score.

**note**

You'll never see these numbers in the game, but the Date score can range from 0 (Horrible) to 1,000 (Dream Date).

At the end of the date, your Sim's date tells you exactly what he or she thought of the experience.

The score at the end of the date determines the final quality of the date and the chances of earning the various rewards.

**note**

The Date score is, more specifically, the composite score of how each event affects both Sims individually. Reactions to events can differ based on who initiated the interaction (usually, the recipient gets less of a relationship boost than the initiator), personality, and Aspiration. Depending on the event, the average or sum of both Sims' reactions to a given event is the amount added to the score.

How an event affects a date depends on the personalities of the Sims involved.

Every event is worth a base score and can affect one, the other, or both Sims on the date. For social interactions between the daters, the number of points is defined by the amount of relationship change caused by the interaction.

How many of the points are awarded, however, depends on three factors:

◆ Each affected Sim's personality

◆ Each affected Sim's Aspiration

◆ Whether or not the social fulfilled a Want or Fear for either or both Sims.

**note**

Keep in mind that the numbers bandied about in this discussion are invisible to you, and knowing the actual amount isn't going to help you have better dates. What is important, however, is understanding the size of the numbers (allowing you to judge which Date Events are big scorers and worth your time and which are potential disasters) and what effect the various bonuses have on them.

## Personality Modifier

Each event score is tied to a personality factor. A Sim on one extreme will react positively and a Sim on the other extreme will react negatively. Let's say, for example, that during a date, Sim A wins a fight with some other Sim (not his date).

This event typically helps a Date score, with a base score of 50 for the Sim who wins the fight and 50 for the other Sim.

The actual amount awarded, however, depends on each Sim's personality. Every Date Event has a bonus score that ranges based on one personality trait. Sims of one extreme get the points on one end of the scale and Sims at the other extreme receive the points at the other end. If a Sim is somewhere between the personality extremes (e.g., Active/Lazy 7), the bonus is proportional within the event's range.

For our victorious fight, the reaction of Sim A is based on his Nice/Grouchy personality with a range of 50 to -50 and the reaction of Sim B is based on Outgoing/Shy with a range of 25 to -25.

◆ If Sim A is Nice/Grouchy 0 (Grouchy), the event gets a bonus of 50 points.

◆ If Sim A is Nice/Grouchy 10 (Nice), the event gets a bonus of -50.

◆ If Sim A is somewhere in between (i.e., Nice/Grouchy 5), the event gets a bonus of 0 (halfway between 50 and -50).

◆ If Sim B is Outgoing/Shy 10 (Outgoing), the event gets a bonus of 25.

◆ If Sim B is Outgoing/Shy 0 (Shy), the event gets a bonus of -25.

◆ If Sim B is somewhere in between (i.e., Outgoing/Shy 5), the event gets a bonus of 0 (halfway between 25 and -25).

**note**

Similar bonuses are given for each Sim's Aspiration, but we'll get to that below.

So, the score for this event will be both Sims' base event scores plus whatever bonus or deduction is made due to their personality. If, therefore, both Sims are inclined to be very happy about this event (A is Grouchy and B is Outgoing), the event will increase the Date score by 100 (each Sim's base score) plus 75 (each Sim's bonus) or 175 points. On the other hand, if both Sims are on the opposite personality extremes, the event would still help the date, but only by 25 points.

There is still another bonus to add (for each Sim's Aspiration) but this example should demonstrate how much the personalities of two Sims can affect how an event impacts their date.

It's important, therefore, to keep in mind your date's and your Sim's personality when choosing activities on a date.

**tip**

You can always approximate your date's personality by asking her about her zodiac sign and consulting the zodiac personality profile table in Chapter 4.

Playing games with a Grouchy Sim can be more trouble than it's worth.

When choosing activities, therefore, consider the possible outcomes. If you know your Sim's date is Grouchy, it's probably best not to waste date time playing a game. If the date were to lose, her personality would make the negative score for losing the game almost twice as bad. A Nice date would still cause a deduction, but it would be minimal and outweighed by your Sim's positive reaction to winning.

## Aspiration Bonus/Penalty

Most Date Events also carry a bonus score awarded based on each Sim's Aspiration. If the Sim has the positive Aspiration, he or she gets points added, if the Sim has the negative Aspiration, he or she gets a reduction. If the Sim has neither Aspiration, the score remains unchanged. These points are in addition to any bonuses for personality traits.

Check out your Sim's date's Aspiration in the Date Meter to decide which events are worth realizing.

Returning to our fight example, both Sims' Aspirations will affect the fight's Date score. If your Sim is a Popularity Sim or the companion is a Family Sim, winning the fight will add 25 points per Sim to the score (base score plus personality bonus). If either your Sim is a Family Sim or the companion is a Popularity Sim, the score will be reduced by -50 points per Sim.

Sim B's Aspiration is always visible on the Date Meter.

## Date Events

> **note**
> In the tables below, your Sim is referred to as Sim A and the Sim's companion is Sim B. If no Sim is specified, the event will score the same for either Sim.

| Date Event | Base Score | Personality + + | Amount | Personality - - | Amount | Aspiration + | Aspiration Bonus | Aspiration - | Aspiration Penalty |
|---|---|---|---|---|---|---|---|---|---|
| Aspiration Desperation (Family) (Sim A) | 0 | Playful | 0 | Serious | 0 | Family, Knowledge | 0 | Romance, Popularity, Pleasure | 0 |
| Aspiration Desperation (Family) (Sim B) | -300 | Playful | 100 | Serious | -200 | Family, Knowledge | 0 | Romance, Popularity, Pleasure | 0 |
| Aspiration Desperation (Grilled Cheese) (Sim A) | 0 | Playful | 0 | Serious | 0 | Grilled Cheese | 0 | None | 0 |
| Aspiration Desperation (Grilled Cheese) (Sim B) | -300 | Playful | 100 | Serious | -200 | Grilled Cheese | 0 | None | 0 |
| Aspiration Desperation (Knowledge) (Sim A) | 0 | Playful | 0 | Serious | 0 | Knowledge | 0 | Romance, Wealth | 0 |
| Aspiration Desperation (Knowledge) (Sim B) | -300 | Playful | 100 | Serious | -200 | Knowledge | 0 | Romance, Wealth | 0 |

## Date Events continued

| DATE EVENT | BASE SCORE | PERSONALITY + + | AMOUNT | PERSONALITY - - | AMOUNT | ASPIRATION + | ASPIRATION BONUS | ASPIRATION - | ASPIRATION PENALTY |
|---|---|---|---|---|---|---|---|---|---|
| Aspiration Desperation (Pleasure) (Sim A) | 0 | Playful | 0 | Serious | 0 | Romance, Wealth, Pleasure, Grilled Cheese | 0 | Family | 0 |
| Aspiration Desperation (Pleasure) (Sim B) | -300 | Playful | 100 | Serious | -200 | Romance, Wealth, Pleasure, Grilled Cheese | 0 | Family | 0 |
| Aspiration Desperation (Popularity) (Sim A) | 0 | Playful | 0 | Serious | 0 | Popularity | 0 | Wealth, Knowledge, Pleasure | 0 |
| Aspiration Desperation (Popularity) (Sim B) | -300 | Playful | 100 | Serious | -200 | Popularity | 0 | Wealth, Knowledge, Pleasure | 0 |
| Aspiration Desperation (Romance) (Sim A) | 0 | Playful | 0 | Serious | 0 | Romance or Popularity | 0 | Family or Knowledge | 0 |
| Aspiration Desperation (Romance) (Sim B) | -300 | Playful | 100 | Serious | -200 | Romance or Popularity | 0 | Family or Knowledge | 0 |
| Aspiration Desperation (Wealth) (Sim A) | 0 | Playful | 0 | Serious | 0 | Wealth, Family, Pleasure, Grilled Cheese | 0 | Popularity | 0 |
| Aspiration Desperation (Wealth) (Sim B) | -300 | Playful | 100 | Serious | -200 | Wealth, Family, Pleasure, Grilled Cheese | 0 | Popularity | 0 |
| Aspiration Failure (Visit from Sim Shrink) | -400 | Playful | 200 | Serious | -200 | Pleasure | 0 | Knowledge | 0 |
| Be Influenced | 25 | Outgoing | 25 | Shy | -25 | Popularity | 10 | Pleasure | -5 |
| Be Jealousy Target | -250 | Outgoing | 100 | Mean | -100 | Romance | 150 | Family | -100 |
| Bite Neck (Sim A) | 200 | Mean | 100 | Nice | -100 | Knowledge | 100 | Family | -50 |
| Bladder Fails (Sim A) | -200 | Sloppy | 200 | Neat | -300 | Family | 0 | Popularity | -500 |
| Bladder Fails (Sim B) | -600 | Sloppy | 200 | Neat | -300 | Family | 100 | Popularity | -500 |
| Crumplebottom - Hit | -250 | Nice | 100 | Mean | -50 | Family | 50 | Romance | -200 |
| Crumplebottom - Lecture | -100 | Nice | 50 | Mean | -100 | Family | 50 | Romance | -200 |
| Crush Relationship Achieved | 100 | Outgoing | 50 | Shy | -50 | Romance | 50 | Knowledge | -50 |
| Crush Relationship Lose | -150 | Nice | 50 | Mean | -50 | Knowledge | 50 | Romance | -50 |
| Dance Sphere Lose Medium (Sim A) | -50 | Lazy | -25 | Active | 25 | Knowledge | 20 | Pleasure | -20 |
| Dance Sphere Lose Medium (Sim B) | -80 | Lazy | -25 | Active | 25 | Knowledge | 20 | Pleasure | -20 |
| Dance Sphere Lose High (Sim A) | -70 | Lazy | -50 | Active | 50 | Knowledge | 20 | Pleasure | -20 |
| Dance Sphere Lose High (Sim B) | -100 | Lazy | -50 | Active | 50 | Knowledge | 20 | Pleasure | -20 |
| Dance Sphere Win Low (Sim A) | 15 | Active | 15 | Lazy | -10 | Pleasure | 10 | Knowledge | -5 |
| Dance Sphere Win Low (Sim B) | 15 | Active | 15 | Lazy | -10 | Pleasure | 10 | Knowledge | -5 |
| Dance Sphere Win Medium (Sim A) | 35 | Active | 25 | Lazy | -25 | Pleasure | 20 | Knowledge | -20 |

## Date Events continued

| Date Event | Base Score | Personality + + | Amount | Personality - - | Amount | Aspiration + | Aspiration Bonus | Aspiration - | Aspiration Penalty |
|---|---|---|---|---|---|---|---|---|---|
| Dance Sphere Win Medium (Sim B) | 35 | Active | 25 | Lazy | -25 | Pleasure | 20 | Knowledge | -20 |
| Dance Sphere Win High (Sim A) | 45 | Active | 25 | Lazy | -25 | Pleasure | 20 | Knowledge | -20 |
| Dance Sphere Win High (Sim B) | 45 | Active | 25 | Lazy | -25 | Pleasure | 20 | Knowledge | -20 |
| Death of Date | -1000 | Nice | 0 | Mean | 0 | Knowledge | 0 | Popularity | 0 |
| Dine Out (Order from Server) | 150 | Playful | 50 | Serious | -50 | Pleasure | 50 | Fortune | -25 |
| Dining Throw Food Accept | 2 | Playful | 15 | Serious | -10 | Pleasure | 15 | Knowledge | -5 |
| Dining Throw Food Reject | 2 | Playful | 10 | Serious | -35 | Pleasure | 5 | Knowledge | -20 |
| Eat Bad Food | 5 | Lazy | 5 | Active | -5 | Knowledge | 0 | Pleasure | -5 |
| Eat Good Food | 50 | Lazy | 25 | Active | -25 | Pleasure | 50 | Knowledge | -10 |
| Energy Fails (Sim A) | -100 | Lazy | 100 | Shy | -100 | Knowledge | 10 | Popularity | -100 |
| Energy Fails (Sim B) | -300 | Playful | 100 | Serious | -200 | Knowledge | 10 | Popularity | -100 |
| Fall Asleep in Food (Sim A) | -150 | Nice | 50 | Mean | -100 | Family | 25 | Popularity | -100 |
| Fight Attack Lose | -150 | Nice | 0 | Mean | -50 | Knowledge | 25 | Popularity | -100 |
| Fight Attack Win | 100 | Mean | 100 | Nice | -300 | Popularity | 50 | Knowledge | -25 |
| Fire | -250 | Playful | 10 | Serious | -35 | Pleasure | 5 | Knowledge | -20 |
| Get Booed (Sim B) | -50 | Outgoing | 25 | Shy | -25 | Knowledge | 10 | Popularity | -25 |
| Get Cheered (Sim B) | 25 | Outgoing | 50 | Shy | -25 | Popularity | 25 | Knowledge | -10 |
| Get Comped Food (Sim A) | 0 | Outgoing | 0 | Shy | 0 | Fortune | 0 | Family | 0 |
| Get Comped Food (Sim B) | 100 | Outgoing | 25 | Shy | -50 | Fortune | 50 | Family | 0 |
| Get Engaged | 10 | Nice | 150 | Mean | -50 | Family | 200 | Romance | -100 |
| Get Engaged Reject | 20 | Nice | 5 | Mean | -100 | Romance | 50 | Family | -100 |
| Get Food Dropped On (Sim A) | -50 | Sloppy | 100 | Neat | -75 | Fortune | 10 | Popularity | -25 |
| Get Food Dropped On (Sim B) | -50 | Sloppy | 100 | Neat | -75 | Fortune | 10 | Popularity | -25 |
| Get Furious (Sim A) | -200 | Nice | 100 | Mean | -200 | Family | 50 | Popularity | -50 |
| Get Married | 10 | Nice | 150 | Mean | -50 | Family | 200 | Romance | -100 |
| Get Married Reject | 20 | Nice | 5 | Mean | -100 | Romance | 50 | Family | -100 |
| Get Pregnant | 200 | Nice | 50 | Mean | -100 | Family | 200 | Romance | -350 |
| Go Broke (Sim A) | -200 | Outgoing | 50 | Shy | -100 | Knowledge | 50 | Fortune | -200 |
| Go Broke (Sim B) | -200 | Outgoing | 50 | Shy | -100 | Knowledge | 50 | Fortune | -200 |
| Go Steady | 4 | Nice | 50 | Mean | -25 | Family | 200 | Romance | -100 |
| Go Steady Reject | 4 | Nice | 50 | Mean | -100 | Romance | 50 | Family | -100 |
| Influences Sim A (Sim B) | 25 | Outgoing | 50 | Shy | -10 | Popularity | 25 | Knowledge | -5 |
| Jealousy | -250 | Nice | 100 | Mean | -100 | Romance | 100 | Family | -100 |
| Lose Fight (Sim A) | -75 | Nice | 25 | Outgoing | -50 | Family | 25 | Popularity | -50 |

# GOING OUT: DATES, GROUPS, AND OUTINGS

## Date Events continued

| Date Event | Base Score | Personality ++ | Amount | Personality -- | Amount | Aspiration + | Aspiration Bonus | Aspiration - | Aspiration Penalty |
|---|---|---|---|---|---|---|---|---|---|
| Lose Fight (Sim B) | -75 | Nice | 25 | Mean | -25 | Family | 25 | Popularity | -50 |
| Love Relationship Achieved | 200 | Outgoing | 50 | Shy | -50 | Romance | 50 | Knowledge | -50 |
| Love Relationship Lost | -200 | Nice | 150 | Mean | -150 | Knowledge | 100 | Romance | -100 |
| Orders Sim B's Liked food (Sim A) | 0 | Lazy | 0 | Active | 0 | Pleasure | 0 | Popularity | 0 |
| Pick Up for Date in Hunka 711 Hwang Motors | 85 | Outgoing | 40 | Shy | -10 | Fortune | 50 | Family | -30 |
| Pick Up for Date in Landwhale by Haevenla | 45 | Shy | 30 | Outgoing | -10 | Family | 50 | Romance | -150 |
| Pick Up for Date in Smoogo Minima | 10 | Sloppy | 20 | Neat | -10 | Knowledge | 10 | Fortune | -30 |
| Pick Up for Date in Smord P328 | 35 | Active | 30 | Lazy | -10 | Pleasure | 20 | Knowledge | -10 |
| Pick Up for Date in Yomoshoto Evasion | 65 | Serious | 30 | Playful | -10 | Knowledge | 20 | Pleasure | -10 |
| Repoman | -400 | Outgoing | 0 | Shy | -100 | Popularity | 0 | Fortune | -200 |
| Save from Death | 300 | Playful | 100 | Serious | -200 | Knowledge | 400 | Family | 0 |
| Say Goodnight to Date w/o Unlocking Time Bonus | -200 | Shy | 0 | Outgoing | -50 | Knowledge | 50 | Romance | -50 |
| Sing Duet | 50 | Playful | 25 | Serious | -25 | Romance | 25 | Knowledge | -25 |
| Skip Out on Check Fail (Sim A) | -200 | Mean | 200 | Nice | -200 | Family | 0 | Fortune | -100 |
| Skip Out on Check Succeed (Sim A) | 0 | Mean | 0 | Nice | 0 | Fortune | 100 | Family | -100 |
| Slow Dance End Unsuccessful | -200 | Nice | 100 | Mean | -50 | Knowledge | 50 | Romance | -100 |
| Smell Bad Reaction | -50 | Sloppy | 50 | Neat | -50 | Knowledge | 25 | Pleasure | -25 |
| Smell Yummy Reaction | 50 | Neat | 25 | Sloppy | -40 | Pleasure | 25 | Knowledge | -10 |
| Smustle Dance Reject | -50 | Lazy | 25 | Active | -25 | Knowledge | 25 | Pleasure | -25 |
| Smustle Dance With Sim B | 50 | Active | 25 | Lazy | -25 | Pleasure | 25 | Knowledge | -25 |
| Social Worker | -700 | Mean | 300 | Nice | -300 | Pleasure | 100 | Family | -500 |
| Streak (Sim B) | 50 | Outgoing | 0 | Shy | 0 | Pleasure | 0 | Knowledge | 0 |
| Talk to Belly (Sim B) | 20 | Nice | 10 | Mean | -10 | Family | 10 | Romance | -10 |
| Throw Up (Sim A) | -100 | Sloppy | 100 | Neat | -250 | Romance | 0 | Pleasure | -100 |
| Throw Up (Sim B) | -100 | Sloppy | 100 | Neat | -250 | Family | 0 | Popularity | -50 |
| Tips Waiter, etc. (Sim B) | 25 | Nice | 45 | Mean | -50 | Fortune | 50 | Knowledge | -25 |
| Use Photo Booth Together | 30 | Outgoing | 40 | Shy | -50 | Popularity | 25 | Fortune | -10 |
| Win Fight (Sim A) | 50 | Outgoing | 25 | Shy | -25 | Family | 25 | Popularity | -50 |
| Win Fight (Sim B) | 50 | Mean | 50 | Nice | -50 | Popularity | 25 | Family | -50 |

The date score impact of the following events are based on changes in Daily and Lifetime Relationship resulting from each interaction. However, instead of the base score being added directly to date score, it is multiplied by the relationship changes on both sides and the resulting number is then added to date score. Note that only a few of these events are further modified by personality or Aspiration—these bonuses, when they occur, are added to the modified base score as with all other date events.

| Date Event | Base Score (Multiplied by rel. change) | Personality + | + Amount | Personality - | - Amount | Aspiration + | Aspiration Bonus | Aspiration - | Aspiration Penalty |
|---|---|---|---|---|---|---|---|---|---|
| Appreciate | 1 | Nice | 0 | Mean | 0 | Family | 0 | Romance | 0 |
| Appreciate Reject | 1 | Mean | 0 | Nice | 0 | Romance | 0 | Family | 0 |
| Booth/Sofa/Bed/HotTub Cuddle | 2 | Outgoing | 20 | Shy | -10 | Romance | 15 | Knowledge | -10 |
| Booth/Sofa/Bed/HotTub Cuddle Reject | 2 | Outgoing | 10 | Shy | -20 | Knowledge | 15 | Romance | -50 |
| Dance Reject | 2 | Lazy | 0 | Active | 0 | Pleasure | 0 | Romance | 0 |
| Dance with Sim | 2 | Active | 0 | Lazy | 0 | Pleasure | 0 | Knowledge | 0 |
| Dining Blow Kiss | 2 | Outgoing | 0 | Shy | 0 | Romance | 0 | Knowledge | 0 |
| Dining Blow Kiss Reject | 2 | Outgoing | 0 | Shy | 0 | Romance | 0 | Knowledge | 0 |
| Dining Feed a Bite | 2 | Nice | 0 | Mean | 0 | Pleasure | 0 | Fortune | 0 |
| Dining Feed a Bite Reject | 2 | Nice | 0 | Mean | 0 | Pleasure | 0 | Fortune | 0 |
| Dining Get Drink Thrown in Face | 2 | Playful | 0 | Serious | 0 | Family | 0 | Popularity | 0 |
| Dining Hold Hands | 2 | Nice | 0 | Mean | 0 | Family | 0 | Knowledge | 0 |
| Dining Hold Hands Reject | 2 | Nice | 0 | Mean | 0 | Family | 0 | Knowledge | 0 |
| Dining Steal A Bite | 2 | Playful | 0 | Serious | 0 | Pleasure | 0 | Fortune | 0 |
| Dining Steal a Bite Reject | 2 | Serious | 0 | Playful | 0 | Fortune | 0 | Pleasure | 0 |
| Dining Throw Drink | 2 | Playful | 0 | Serious | 0 | Family | 0 | Knowledge | 0 |
| Entertain | 1 | Outgoing | 0 | Shy | 0 | Popularity | 0 | Knowledge | 0 |
| Entertain Reject | 1 | Shy | 0 | Outgoing | 0 | Knowledge | 0 | Popularity | 0 |
| Fight | 3 | Mean | 0 | Nice | 0 | Popularity | 0 | Knowledge | 0 |
| Flirt | 2 | Playful | 0 | Serious | 0 | Pleasure | 0 | Family | 0 |
| Flirt Reject | 2 | Serious | 0 | Playful | 0 | Family | 0 | Pleasure | 0 |
| Get Bitten By Vampire | 3 | Playful | 25 | Serious | -25 | Knowledge | 200 | Family | -50 |
| Get Engaged | 10 | Nice | 150 | Mean | -50 | Family | 200 | Romance | -100 |
| Get Engaged Reject | 20 | Nice | 5 | Mean | -100 | Romance | 50 | Family | -100 |
| Get Married | 10 | Nice | 150 | Mean | -50 | Family | 200 | Romance | -100 |
| Get Married Reject | 20 | Nice | 5 | Mean | -100 | Romance | 50 | Family | -100 |
| Go Steady | 4 | Nice | 50 | Mean | -25 | Family | 200 | Romance | -100 |
| Go Steady Reject | 4 | Nice | 50 | Mean | -100 | Romance | 50 | Family | -100 |
| Hug | 2 | Nice | 0 | Mean | 0 | Family | 0 | Fortune | 0 |

# GOING OUT: DATES, GROUPS, AND OUTINGS

| Date Event | Base Score (Multiplied by Rel. Change) | Personality + | + Amount | Personality - | - Amount | Aspiration + | Aspiration Bonus | Aspiration - | Aspiration Penalty |
|---|---|---|---|---|---|---|---|---|---|
| Hug Reject | 2 | Mean | 0 | Nice | 0 | Fortune | 0 | Family | 0 |
| Irritate | 1 | Nice | 0 | Mean | 0 | Popularity | 0 | Family | 0 |
| Kiss Accept | 2 | Outgoing | 0 | Shy | 0 | Romance | 0 | Knowledge | 0 |
| Kiss Reject | 2 | Shy | 0 | Outgoing | 0 | Knowledge | 0 | Romance | 0 |
| Lose Game (Sim A) | 1 | Nice | 0 | Mean | 0 | Family | 0 | Popularity | 0 |
| Lose Game (Sim B) | 1 | Nice | 0 | Mean | 0 | Family | 0 | Popularity | 0 |
| Play | 1 | Playful | 0 | Serious | 0 | Pleasure | 0 | Fortune | 0 |
| Play Reject | 1 | Serious | 0 | Playful | 0 | Fortune | 0 | Pleasure | 0 |
| Prank | 1 | Playful | 0 | Serious | 0 | Popularity | 0 | Knowledge | 0 |
| Prank Reject | 1 | Serious | 0 | Playful | 0 | Knowledge | 0 | Popularity | 0 |
| School Cheer | 1 | Playful | 0 | Serious | 0 | Knowledge | 0 | Romance | 0 |
| Secret Handshake | 1 | Outgoing | 0 | Shy | 0 | Knowledge | 0 | Family | 0 |
| Secret Handshake Reject | 1 | Shy | 0 | Outgoing | 0 | Family | 0 | Knowledge | 0 |
| Slow Dance Reject | 2 | Nice | 0 | Mean | 0 | Knowledge | 0 | Romance | 0 |
| Slow Dance Step on Foot | 2 | Nice | 0 | Mean | 0 | Family | 0 | Popularity | 0 |
| Slow Dance With Sim | 2 | Nice | 0 | Mean | 0 | Romance | 0 | Knowledge | 0 |
| Slow Dance Nested | 2 | Nice | 0 | Mean | 0 | Romance | 0 | Knowledge | 0 |
| Slow Dance Nested Reject | 2 | Nice | 0 | Mean | 0 | Knowledge | 0 | Romance | 0 |
| Talk | 1 | Outgoing | 0 | Shy | 0 | Knowledge | 0 | Romance | 0 |
| Talk Reject | 1 | Shy | 0 | Outgoing | 0 | Romance | 0 | Knowledge | 0 |
| Win Game (Sim A) | 1 | Playful | 0 | Serious | 0 | Popularity | 0 | Romance | 0 |
| Win Game (Sim B) | 1 | Playful | 0 | Serious | 0 | Knowledge | 0 | Popularity | 0 |
| WooHoo | 5 | Outgoing | 0 | Shy | 0 | Romance | 0 | Knowledge | 0 |
| WooHoo Reject | 5 | Shy | 0 | Outgoing | 0 | Knowledge | 0 | Romance | 0 |

**note**

While on a date, the bulk of a Sim's Wants and Fears will be directly related to the date rather than the usual more diffuse Aspiration-driven forces.

Click on the companion's Aspiration icon in the Date Meter to reveal his or her current Wants.

Keep an eye on your Sim's and the companion's Wants. If the companion is showing a Want, it's likely because it will score well with him or her based on his or her personality and Aspiration. Likewise, your Sim's Wants during a date favor actions likely to achieve the highest scores. What's more, every Aspiration your Sim and the date gain or lose translates into a fraction of a Date point (1/20th to be exact); if, for example, the companion satisfies a 1,000 point Want, Date score will rise by 50 points.

**note**

See a companion's Wants by clicking on his or her Aspiration icon on the Date Meter.

## Time

Dates are timed events, but the time remaining can change based on the Date score.

When you begin a date, the timer begins counting down from three minutes.

When the timer shifts to red, you better elevate the Date score fast.

This does not mean you have three minutes in the entire date; it means you have three minutes to get to the next highest scoring level.

When the next scoring level is reached (say, from Lame to Good), more time is added to the clock. Reach the next threshold and another time bonus is awarded. When you get to the top tier (Dream Date), there are no more time bonuses and the date will end when the timer runs out. Less bonus time is awarded for each higher Date Level, so reaching the highest levels becomes progressively more challenging.

**note**

If you suffer a slide in Date score and drop below your current Date Level, you won't get a time bonus for crossing the line again. The next time bonus won't come until you rise to the next highest tier.

Thus, it's very important to make good use of your time on a date. The longer you take to get to each level, the less time you'll have to reach the following time bonus.

### Date Time Bonuses

| Date Level Achieved | Time Bonus |
|---|---|
| Good | 2:30 |
| Great | 2:00 |
| Dream | 0:90 |

**note**

Ending a date by saying good-bye without having unlocked any higher levels is a negative Date Event and carries an extra reduction in score. Shy and Knowledge Sims are more forgiving of this and Outgoing and Romance Sims look upon it even more harshly.

## Initial Date Score

All dates begin at the same initial score, just above the Okay level.

**tip**

Leaving for a date in the date's personality/Aspiration-preferred car is a Date Event and provides an increase in Date points before your Sim reaches the Community Lot. This isn't, literally, a difference in initial Date score but an off-screen scoring opportunity. The effect is, however, the same.

## Reaching a New Date Level

Every time a date rises to a new Date Level, two things happen:

◆ Time is extended by a variable amount (less time for higher levels)

◆ Both Sims' Needs are given a boost

The latter reward helps extend the date and keep the Sims focused on enjoying themselves, liberating them from tending to their basic Needs.

## Changing Lots While on a Date

During a date, you can change lots (with one exception) any time you please. Your date will follow you to any other Community Lot, and no travel time counts against the Date Timer.

A date on a Community Lot can't return to your Sim's home unless relationship is high enough to successfully do the Ask...Back to My Place interaction.

The one place you can't go from a Community Lot date is back to your Sim's own home because doing this ends the date.

This isn't to say you can't move a date to your Sim's home lot. To do this, select the Ask...Back to My Place social. The other Sim will either accept or reject based on Mood, Outgoing/Shy or Nice/Grouchy, and Daily and Lifetime Relationship.

If the other Sim accepts, the date moves to your Sim's home lot and continues normally.

## Ending a Date

Dates can be ended in a variety of ways, not all of them graceful:

◆ Score timer reaches 0: Date score is final and date ends.

◆ Score reaches 0 (bottom of Horrible): Date ends immediately with worst possible score and both Sims get a dramatic depletion of their Needs. Sim B delivers a stern lecture.

◆ End the Date: Using this interaction, both Sims agree to call it a day at the current final score. If you haven't won any extended time yet, this is a negative Date Event that will drop the score. If you have unlocked at least one time extension, there is no penalty for ending a date in this way.

◆ Ask...Do You Want a Ride Home?: Functions the same as End the Date but both Sims go to taxi or Sim's car and leave lot together. Your Sim then arrives back at his or her home lot alone (having already dropped off the date). As with End the Date, you only receive a penalty for ending the date this way if you haven't yet unlocked any time extensions.

◆ Ask...Back to My Place: If this interaction is rejected, the date ends immediately at its current score and Sim B leaves the lot. If, on the other hand, the invitation is accepted, both Sims retire to car or taxi, transition to your Sim's home lot, and continue the date there. This is the *only* way to move a date to your Sim's home lot from any other lot without ending the date.

◆ Asking Another Sim for a Date: During a date you are free (although it's uncouth) to ask another Sim for a date, but this has severe consequences for your current date and even the new one. The Date score will drop and there's an additional Daily and Lifetime Relationship drop caused by the date switch. The ditched Sim may also react jealously (according to the usual rules) against both your Sim and his or her new companion (this can harm the score for the new date).

◆ Outside forces end the date prematurely: If your date's motives drop too low, your Sim departs for work or school, or your Sim's companion dies, the date ends at its current state with no penalties save any score changes resulting from the event itself. If, for example, your date is killed by a falling satellite while stargazing, this would end the date at its current score, minus the substantial penalty for date death.

Switching dates is extremely bad form, but we suppose you have your reasons. Never mind the trail of broken hearts you'll leave in your Sim's wake.

**tip**

If a date does die, the date isn't ended until after the Grim Reaper departs the lot. Thus, if the manner of death allows for pleading for the deceased's life, there is time to do so before the date ends. If your Sim successfully pleads for the date's restoration, that too is a Date Event that mitigates the damage of the death.

## Final Date Score and Rewards

The score at the end of the date determines what happens next. The final Date score is the Date Level at the moment the date ends, ranging from:

◆ Dream Date (950–1,000)
◆ Great (650–950)
◆ Good (425–650)
◆ Okay (300–425)
◆ Lame (200–300)
◆ Bad (100–200)
◆ Horrible (0–100)

At the conclusion of the date, the Sims bid farewell. How they do this depends on how the date went:

◆ Dream Date: Romantic Kiss
◆ Great: Tender Kiss
◆ Good: Peck
◆ Okay: Hug
◆ Lame: Shrug/Sigh
◆ Bad: Lecture
◆ Horrible: Yell At/Poke/Shove

Additionally, the outcome of the date can have up to three effects on the dating Sims:

1. **Needs:** Positive dates result in a proportional boost in all Needs—the higher the score the larger the boost. Negative dates result in a depletion of all Needs, again in proportion to the Date score.

2. **Relationship:** In addition to any relationship gains/losses on the date, both Sims receive a proportional boost or drop in both Daily and Lifetime Relationship toward each other. The higher the score, the larger the boost.

3. **Memory:** Dream, Great, Bad, and Horrible dates generate a memory that your Sim can dream, think, or talk about.

**note**

Additionally, the outcome of the date may, depending on the score, fulfill a Want or realize a Fear (e.g., Fear: Have a bad date with so-and-so).

These, of course, are just the immediate benefits/penalties for a date. Next come the aftereffects.

**note**

Many but not all of these rewards are also given for outings (see Outings, below).

## Date Rewards

The effects of a date last beyond the encounter itself. Depending on how well the date went, several good and some bad results can arrive as late as the following day. At least one will make your Sims think twice about ever cheating on a date again.

## Reward Objects

The quality of a date dictates what, if anything your Sim will receive the next day.

After a date, your Sim may receive a delivery from the other Sim. What it is, however, depends on how the date went:

If things go poorly on your date, those aren't flowers on your Sim's doorstep. That smell is never coming out!

◆ **Dream Date:** Dated Sim drops by and delivers a bouquet of flowers. These flowers can be placed in the home; they're artificial and will never die.

◆ **Great Date:** Dated Sim drops by and delivers a single flower. This flower can be placed in the home; it's artificial and will never die.

◆ **Good Date:** The postal worker delivers a love letter from the date. Once your Sim removes it from the mailbox, it goes into the Sim's inventory where it (emblazoned with the sender's picture) can be inspected. The letter can be removed from inventory and placed for display on mantles, walls, or surfaces. If another Sim who has a romantic relationship with the recipient sees the displayed letter, he or she will react jealously.

◆ **Okay Date:** No reward

◆ **Lame Date:** No reward

◆ **Bad Date:** The postal worker delivers a hate letter from the date. Once your Sim removes it from the mailbox, it goes into the

Sim's inventory where it (emblazoned with the sender's picture) can be inspected. Letter can be removed from inventory and placed for display on mantles, walls, or surfaces.

◆ **Horrible Date:** The date sneaks onto your Sim's lot and deposits a flaming bag of poo at the door. This object does not cause fires and will burn infinitely until either stomped out (putting out the flames but depleting your Sim's Hygiene) or placed in your Sim's inventory. There's a slim chance your Sim could catch fire while stomping on the bag of poo, but it won't spread to anything else. Dispose of the bag of poo by stomping and sweeping up the ashes; it can't be sold.

**note**
Love and hate letters can be displayed in your Sim's home.

**note**
Yes, the flaming bag of poo can be placed in your Sim's inventory in either its flaming or non-flaming state. Collect a few and use them like luminarias at your Sims' next outdoor party. It'll be kind of a depressing party, but still.

## Insta-Promotion

If a Sim's date is employed at a higher level in the same career track (above level 3), there's a chance that the date will pull some strings and the Sim will receive a promotion the next time he or she goes to work.

The chance of this happening rises with:

◆ The quality of the date
◆ The dated Sim's job level

If both Sims on a date are from the same household, no promotions will be offered.

If your Sim's date is in the same career track but in a higher job, there's a chance he or she will get your Sim a promotion.

To discover if a Sim is in your Sim's career track and at what level, use the Ask…What's Your Job? interaction.

## Restaurant Coupon

If a date involved dining at a restaurant, there's a chance that the next day's mail will bring a coupon for a free meal at any restaurant.

The chance of receiving this reward rises with the quality of the date.

Whoever takes this letter out of the mailbox (even if not the Sim who went on the date) puts it in his or her inventory and can use it at will.

**tip**

If you wish to move a coupon from the inventory of one Sim to another, drop it on the ground and pick it up with the other Sim.

If a Sim has a restaurant coupon in his or her inventory, you can choose to use it when you click on the host podium to pay for the meal. In addition to the usual options, you may "Use Coupon." The coupon will cover any meal no matter how big the bill.

## Skill Point Award

It always pays to associate with the right people, people of achievement and drive. As such, other Sims can be a good influence on your Sim's skills.

**note**

Unlike promotions, skill point increases can come from Sims in your Sim's household.

Inquire about a Sim's skills to see if a skill boost might be in the near future.

After a date, your Sim may receive a skill level increase in one or more skill. You may even be promoted more than one level in a single skill.

Each time Date Level increases to a new height (e.g., Good to Great), there's a chance to get a point in each skill. Every time a new level is reached, you get another opportunity to gain skill.

**note**

No skill points are awarded when you increase to a threshold you had attained but lost. The next skill point won't come until you reach the next highest unattained Date Level.

Also, you won't *lose* skill points—either your Sim's own or any won during the date—no matter how badly the date is going.

These points are not announced or added until the end of the date. At that time, every skill level you gained will be added to your Sim.

The chance of a skill award increases with the Date score.

You can discover your companion's skill levels by using the Ask...What Are Your Skills? interaction. The Sim reveals his high-ranking skills in the following terms:

◆ "I'm pretty good at...": skill 1–3

◆ "I'm very good at...": skill 4–7

◆ "I'm an expert at...": skill 8–10

If the asked Sim has no skills, he or she will say "I'm not really good at anything yet." If the Sim is successful at multiple skills, they will be listed. For example: "I'm very good at: Mechanical, Body."

## Another Date

One good date leads to another.

The day after a successful date, the date may telephone to invite your Sim on another date. If accepted, the date begins and your Sim has one hour to leave for a Community Lot of your choosing.

## Contacts (a.k.a. "The Friend of a Friend")

Having good dates (or outings) can expand your Sim's social circle even after the outing's over.

The day after a successful date or outing, your Sim may get a call from an unknown Sim who identifies him- or herself as being a friend of someone on the previous outing. The caller invites your Sim to an outing with a group selected randomly from the caller's groups or assembled from randomly chosen downtownies.

The mutual friend named by the caller will also attend.

**note**
Find further information about contacts Chapter 9.

Contacts are valuable because they are temporary friends even before your Sim actually meets them. Thus, during their limited time as a contact—depending on the Date or Outing score that caused them to call—they count toward your Sim's friend count for both career and influence. When the contact's timer runs out, that Sim no longer counts toward these totals, unless your Sim befriended him or her in the normal way in the meantime; however, the contact does stay in your Sim's Relationship panel with whatever of their initial Daily/Lifetime Relationship score remains.

**note**
The lifetime of a contact depends on how well the previous date went:

◆ Okay: 12 hours

◆ Good: 24 hours

◆ Great: 48 hours

◆ Dream Date: 52 hours

## Surprise Gift

Shortly after a high-scoring date (Good or higher), you may get a little surprise. There's a chance the date will sneak onto your Sim's lot and drop off a free object.

What they drop off depends on the final score. The object is chosen at random from the list for each score level. The higher the score, the more valuable the object. A Dream Date can deliver a piano or an expensive stereo while a Good date will bring a garden gnome or a remote-controlled car.

# Groups and Outings

Traditionally, Sims could invite over individual Sims or ask to meet a single Sim at a Community Lot. Every now and then, invited guests brought a friend along or your Sim could tote along a few members of his or her household. But, you could never arrange an outing of Sims from various households or invite over a large gathering without throwing a party.

With groups and outings, it's now possible to do all this. You can even undertake scored outings for a wide variety of rewards.

## Groups

A group is a defined collection of Sims identified by a group name. Such Sims can be called and summoned by group name rather than individually and often a group will, through one of its members, invite your Sim out for a gathering.

Once defined, a group can be accessed or edited by any playable Sim in the group. Thus, if you use a Sim in one household to create the group and include a playable Sim (marked by a green plumb bob in the Manage Group menu) from another household, the second Sim can be used to invite the group for outings, edit the group, or delete it entirely. He or she will also receive occasional outing invitations from the group.

## Kinds of Groups

There are two kinds of groups, defined by how they're assembled:

◆ Managed Groups     ◆ Casual Groups

### Managed Groups

The Manage Group menu is accessed via the telephone.

Use any house or mobile phone and select the Groups... menu. In Manage Groups, you can select which Sims to add to (or remove from) the group (from the pool of Sims known to your Sim).

Once created, the group appears in the groups available to every playable Sim in the group.

**note**

If a townie later becomes a playable Sim (via marriage or becoming a roomie), they too will have the power to manage and invite the group.

Regardless of which Sim(s) created or can manage the group, no two groups in a base neighborhood or any of its attendant downtowns or universities can have the same group name.

**note**

No matter the kind of group, all group members (except the currently selected Sim) will have small blue plumb bobs over their heads. These indicators show their membership in the group but do not change color to reflect their Mood. If more than one member of a group is a playable Sim, switching to a different one changes them to a normal plumb bob and the previously controlled Sim swaps his normal one for a blue group plumb bob.

Sometimes, members of a group will bag on an invitation for various reasons.

Inviting a group doesn't guarantee all members will be able to attend. Group members decide to attend based on the same factors as individual Sims invited over in the traditional way (based on Daily Relationship, whether they're asleep or at work at the time of the call, and whether they have phones in their homes). If any group members decline, you'll be informed immediately who begged off and why.

**note**
The size of your groups may be limited by your computer's performance.

## Casual Groups

Casual groups are created in-person and individually through the Ask...to Form Casual Group interaction. The recipient can either accept or reject the invitation based on Daily Relationship and either Mood or Lifetime Relationship.

Casual groups are improvised groups, made up of whatever Sims present you wish to ask.

Casual groups can be assembled for either Just for Fun (unscored gatherings) or For an Outing (scored/timed with a chance of rewards, like dates). You can make this choice when you invite the first member of the group.

Once formed, casual groups behave identically to managed groups.

## Adding or Removing Group Members

While a group is assembled, you can add or remove any Sim from the group.

To remove a single group member from the current outing (not, mind you, from a managed group membership), use the Ask...To Leave Group interaction. The removed Sim may remain on the lot after being dismissed but won't follow or contribute to the score of the group. If the Sim is playable, he or she will remain playable but act independently of the group.

To add any Sim on the lot to a group (either casual or scored gatherings), use the Ask...To Join Group interaction. If the outing is for a managed group, the new Sim is added to the outing only, not the group list.

## Autonomous Quitting Groups

If any individual group member's Needs or Mood deplete too low, that Sim excuses him- or herself

from the group and departs the lot (just as he or she would if he or she were visiting your Sim's home).

To avoid defections, give your group periods of freedom to tend to their Needs. If you dominate their movements by constantly engaging in activities they'll feel compelled to watch or join, they'll bail out of the group sooner.

A just-for-fun gathering looks just like an outing except there's no score meter.

**note**
When grouped Sims disperse around a lot, you can call them all back to your Sim with the Gather Group self-interaction.

## Disbanding Groups

To disband a casual group, use the End Casual Group self-interaction on any controllable group member. This gathers all the group members and the selected Sim wishes them farewell. The removed Sims may remain on the lot after being dismissed; any playable Sims in the erstwhile group remain playable.

A scored outing is ended in the same manner. The final score for the outing is awarded when the outing is disbanded. Unlike prematurely ended dates, there are no score or Need penalties for ending an outing that's going poorly.

# Kinds of Group Gathering

There are two kinds of group gatherings:
♦ Unscored Gatherings (called "Just for Fun")
♦ Scored Gatherings (called "Outings")

## Just for Fun Gatherings

Groups can be summoned or assembled for unscored just-for-fun excursions, either at a Sim's home or on a Community Lot.

Just-for-fun gatherings stay together for as long as the group members can maintain their Needs and Mood. As with any other gathering, the members follow any playable Sim from lot to lot (including to the playable Sim's home lot) and join and watch his or her activities. Unscored groups are particularly useful for having Sims be seated at the same table in restaurants; even if Sims arrive at a lot together, they won't dine together unless they're in either a date or group.

When you wish to end the just-for-fun gathering, select the End Group interaction on any playable Sim.

## Outings

Outings are scored gatherings that begin either at a Sim's home or on a Community Lot. The can be initiated either by phone call to a managed group or ad hoc by assembling a casual group.

**note**
The first time you play any household after installing this expansion pack, you get an opportunity for an outing. Within the first few hours, your Sim receives a call from a friend or a random townie inviting them downtown as part of a group. You can choose to go by accepting the invitation.

Outings are scored based on several factors including Mood, relationship changes, Outing Events, and Aspiration points.

The Outing Meter appears in the upper right corner, just like the Date Meter.

**note**

Scored outings always start just above the line between Boring and So-So. Whenever a new member is added to the outing, his or her contribution to the score always starts at this point. Therefore, adding new members to the group can drastically affect the total score.

High-scoring outings can have several possible rewards (see "Outing Rewards," below).

## Gathering Locations

Gatherings can be assembled in either of two places:

◆ At home
◆ On a Community Lot

### At Home Gatherings

Gatherings held at your Sim's home are convened by house or cell phone using the Groups…Invite Group Over… interaction.

Casual home gatherings are a great way to have a bunch of Sims over without the pressure of a Party score.

Home gatherings can be done either Just for Fun or For an Outing. Once convened, however, the group can be moved to any Community Lot by calling a taxi or using your Sim's private car.

After inviting a group, the members will show up a few moments later. Greet them to continue the gathering.

## Community Lot Gatherings

Group gatherings can be started on Community Lots by using the Groups…Meet Group on Community Lot…interaction on any house or cell phone.

Choose the mode of transportation, then decide where to go.

Select whether the venture is to be Just for Fun or For an Outing. Next, if the household has a car, decide if you want to go by taxi or car. Either way, choose your destination and you're off. The attending members of the group will arrive with your Sim at the Community Lot (they were picked up on the way).

Community Lot gatherings can move to any other Community Lot or back to your Sim's home lot.

**note**

All Sim cars have infinite seating, so you can drive to a gathering no matter how many Sims are invited.

## Scoring Outings

Outings are scored similarly to dates but with other factors involved.

**note**

The Outing Meter is very similar to the Date Meter but lacks the picture/Aspiration of any Sim on the outing and provides no access to anyone else's Wants and Fears. To learn those on an outing, you must use the Ask...What Do You Want? and Ask...What Do You Fear? interactions.

Outing score ranges from:

◆ Rockin' (950–1,000)
◆ Super (650–950)
◆ Fun (425–650)
◆ So-So (300–425)
◆ Boring (200–300)
◆ A Real Drag (100–200)
◆ Disaster (0–100)

Points are awarded for:

◆ Average group Mood
◆ Relationship changes
◆ Outing Events
◆ Aspiration points gained and lost as a result of fulfilled Wants and Fears

## Average Group Mood

The average Mood of all the group members is taken at the beginning of an outing, then rechecked regularly. Throughout the outing, any changes up or down from the previous check will generate an increase or decrease in Outing points.

## Relationship Changes

Any changes in relationship between group members during the outing increase or decrease Outing score.

**note**

This element functions just like scoring for parties.

## Outing Events

Outing Events work identically to Date Events, deducting or adding points for the occurrence of specified events. The score for each occurrence is modified by:

◆ Each Sim's personality
◆ Each Sim's Aspiration

Thus, any defined event scores differently based on each Sim's individual personality and Aspiration. The average of all group members' reactions to an event is added to the Outing score.

Though the mechanism and scoring are similar to dates, there are fewer Outing Events. Outing score is changed by:

- Appreciate
- Appreciate Reject
- Aspiration Failure (Shrink)
- Be Influenced
- Be Jealousy Target
- Booth/Sofa/Bed/Hot Tub Cuddle
- Booth/Sofa/Bed/Hot Tub Cuddle Reject
- Crumplebottom (Hit)
- Crumplebottom (Lecture)
- Dance Reject
- Dance Sphere Lose High
- Dance Sphere Lose Medium
- Dance Sphere Win High
- Dance Sphere Win Low
- Dance Sphere Win Medium
- Dance with Sim
- Date Influences Sim
- Death of Date
- Dine Out (Order from Server)
- Dining Blow Kiss
- Dining Blow Kiss Reject
- Dining Feed a Bite
- Dining Feed a Bite Reject
- Dining Get Drink Thrown in Face
- Dining Hold Hands
- Dining Hold Hands Reject
- Dining Steal a Bite Reject
- Dining Steal A Bite
- Dining Throw Drink
- Dining Throw Food Accept
- Dining Throw Food Reject
- Eat Bad Food
- Eat Good Food
- Energy Failure
- Entertain
- Entertain Reject
- Fall Asleep in Food
- Fight
- Fight Attack Lose
- Fight Attack Win
- Flirt
- Flirt Reject
- Gain Aspiration Points
- Get Comped Food
- Get Engaged
- Get Engaged Reject
- Get Furious
- Get Married
- Get Married Reject
- Get Pregnant
- Go Steady
- Go Steady Reject
- Hug
- Hug Reject
- Irritate
- Jealousy
- Kiss
- Kiss Reject
- Play
- Play Reject
- Prank
- Prank Reject
- Repoman
- Save from Death
- School Cheer
- Secret Handshake
- Secret Handshake Reject
- Sim Dance Sphere Lose High
- Sim Dance Sphere Lose Medium
- Sim Dance Sphere Win High
- Sim Dance Sphere Win Low
- Sim Dance Sphere Win Medium
- Sing Duet
- Slow Dance End Unsuccessful
- Slow Dance Reject
- Slow Dance Nested
- Slow Dance Nested Reject
- Slow Dance Step on Foot
- Slow Dance With Sim
- Smell Bad Reaction
- Smell Yummy Reaction
- Smustle Dance With Sim
- Social Worker
- Talk
- Talk Reject
- Use Photo Booth Together
- Vampire-Bite Neck
- Vampire-Get Bitten
- WooHoo
- WooHoo Reject

There are also a few events that are exclusive to outings. If any of the relationships listed below are achieved during an outing, that event will affect the outing score:

| Date Event | Base Score | Personality + + Amount | Personality - - Amount | Aspiration + | Aspiration Bonus | Aspiration - | Aspiration Penalty |
|---|---|---|---|---|---|---|---|
| Achieve Best Friend Relationship | 200 | Outgoing | 50 | Shy | -50 | Romance | 50 | Knowledge | -50 |
| Lose Best Friend Relationship | -200 | Nice | 150 | Mean | -150 | Knowledge | 100 | Romance | -100 |
| Achieve Friend Relationship | 100 | Outgoing | 50 | Shy | -50 | Romance | 50 | Knowledge | -50 |
| Lose Friend Relationship | -150 | Nice | 50 | Mean | -50 | Knowledge | 50 | Romance | -50 |

## Scoring Effects

Whenever the outing score crosses up or down into a new scoring zone (even one already achieved), all group members receive a boost or drop in their Needs.

Also, as with dates, any rise into a heretofore unattained scoring level awards a time extension to the outing. To get a further time extension, raise Outing score to the next highest level before the clock expires.

## Outing Rewards

When an outing ends, there are several possible rewards for your Sim.

### Future Invitations

If your Sim had a high scoring outing with a group, there's a chance a member of the group may call the next day to invite him or her on another outing. Generally, the caller will be the member of the group with the highest Daily Relationship to your Sim.

The group for which the Sim is inviting, however, may not be the same group from the past. If the caller is the member of multiple groups, which of those groups he or she "represents" is chosen randomly. If the original group was a casual group and the caller is not a member of any managed group, the outing will be attended by the caller and a randomly selected gang of downtownies.

### Contacts (a.k.a. "The Friend of a Friend")

Having good outings can expand your Sim's social circle even after the outing's over.

This works exactly the same as with dates.

**note**

The lifetime of a contact depends on how well the previous outing went:

◆ So-So: 12 hours

◆ Fun: 24 hours

◆ Super: 48 hours

◆ Rockin': 52 hours

### Insta-Promotion

A Sim fresh off an outing with a Sim in the same career track may receive a promotion courtesy of the higher-ranking Sim.

This works in the same way as it does with dates, though the larger number of Sims in the average outing can increase the chances of promotion. Because each Sim on the outing who ranks higher in your Sim's career track (above Level 3) has a chance of offering a promotion, the more Sims in the group who qualify, the more likely the reward.

See "Date Rewards," above, for details.

### Restaurant Coupon

After an outing, a Sim may receive a coupon for a free dinner on a Community Lot in his mailbox. See "Date Rewards," above, for details.

### Skill Point Award

When an outing ends, your Sim can receive one or more increases in one or more of his or her skills. This works largely the same as it does on dates, but there are some important added factors.

Every time your outing score rises into a new level (e.g., from Fun to Super), there's a chance that your Sim could gain one point in one or more of his or her skills. The chances of this happening are random, but the likelihood rises the more total skill points there are in the rest of the group. Thus a group of five Sims, each with 9 Creativity points, will offer a better chance of gaining a Creativity point than five Sims each with 7 Creativity. Because the odds rise with the total number of points in the group rather than the average, the number of Sims on the outing matters; the more Sims, the better the odds.

As a result, the odds of gaining skill points after outings are much better than after a date (which is only ever with one other Sim).

You can discover your companions' skill levels by using the Ask…What Are Your Skills? interaction.

## Surprise Gift

A good outing can nab you a very expensive present from a member of the group.

This works identically as it does after a date.

## Converting to a Date

If, as often happens, love begins to bloom on an outing, you can convert the outing with a group into a date with one of the group's members. Use the Ask…On Date interaction to make the transition, but be aware of the consequences.

If there is more than one playable Sim in the group, the outing will go on without the now-dating Sim. Thus, you'll be playing both a date and an outing simultaneously depending on which playable Sim is active.

If the Sim that switches to a date is the last playable Sim on the outing, the outing disbands immediately at its current score.

## Dining Out

There's nothing like a home-cooked meal, but when a Sim yearns to go out on the town, he or she wants to settle in at a nice restaurant to be served a professionally cooked meal. Now he or she can.

Restaurants can exist on any Community Lot and most lots in Downtown have at least a modest food service.

## Beginning the Dining Experience

The host podium is the start of the dining process.

To begin the dining experience, click on the host podium (or the NPC Host) and select "Be Seated" or "Be Seated at Counter."

### note

If any part of the restaurant system (e.g., tables, chairs, or the kitchen stove) is missing from the lot, the restaurant will be closed with an "under construction" sign on the door. Enter the lot in Build mode to add any missing objects.

The NPC Host will show you to your seats. If your Sim is part of a date or a group, every effort will be made to seat the group at the same table:

◆ If two Sims arrive at the lot together but aren't on a date or part of a group, only the Sim that requested the table will be seated.

◆ If two Sims are on a date, they'll be seated together, preferably side by side.

◆ If up to eight Sims arrive as a group and there is a large enough table, they'll be seated together.

◆ If any large group arrives and no one table will hold them, the party will be split into no more than two tables. If possible the Host will seat your Sim with the group members with whom he has the highest relationship.

◆ If the group is too large for two tables or there is no available seating, the Host will apologetically refuse to seat the group.

Sims don't have to sit at a table: the counter's open too.

If Sims ask to be seated at the counter, the Host attempts to seat them contiguously. If that's impossible, the group will be scattered but will still behave conversationally as if seated together. They will not, however, be able to do any counter interactions unless seated side by side.

## Relationship with the Staff

Building a strong relationship with restaurant Hosts and Servers can be extremely beneficial.

Because Hosts are so busy at the restaurant, the best time to socialize with them is away from work. Once met, they can be included in groups or invited over for more productive relationship building.

The Host has the power to deduct (or "comp") part or all of your Sim's meal. The chances of this and the percentage of the meal that can be comped increase with relationship with the Host.

### tip

There's no need to visit the restaurant to build relationship with Servers and Hosts. Once you meet them, invite them to your Sim's home, include them in groups and dates and socialize with them in any way possible. With a sturdy relationship in place, your next visit to the same restaurant may be considerably cheaper.

Good relations with the Host also mean a warm greeting.

Relationship with a Server benefits you in a different way: avoidance of embarrassment. The better your relationship with a given Server, the lower the chances he or she will accidentally drop food on your Sim. Having a negative relationship with a Server heightens the chances of this indignity.

### note

Each restaurant has a battery of regular Servers and Hosts, though there's no guarantee that any particular one be working when your Sim visits or serving your Sim's table. Thus, the more you visit, the more Servers and Hosts you can befriend and the better your chances of getting a comped meal.

Hostile Servers can get pretty clumsy around Sims they dislike.

### tip

Getting a comped meal is a positive Date Event, particularly impressing Fortune Aspiration and Outgoing Sims.

## Ordering

### note

Every Sim has a randomly assigned favorite food. This favorite is permanent and unchangeable and every Sim will order his or her favorite dish when left to his or her own devices. If your Sim orders his or her date's favorite food, that Sim will be very pleased, thus improving Date score. Pleasure Aspiration and Lazy Sims like this best of all, providing even higher boosts to Date score. Pay attention to your date's thought balloon as he or she reads the menu to see what his or her favorite food is.

Chat up the Server for a bit before ordering.

Once your Sim is seated, the NPC Server visits the table to take the order.

### tip

Unless your Sim is on a date and time is tight, hold off on ordering and let your Sim automatically converse with the Server before ordering. Building relationship with the Server reduces the chances of having food spilled on your Sim.

The Server stands at your Sims' table and awaits your order, conversing to fill the time. Once you're ready to order, click on the Server and select how you want to order. If the Server wanders away, click on him or her and choose "Order."

You have several options when ordering. You may:

◆ Order for Me: Order any item on the menu for your Sim.

◆ Order for [Other Sim's Name]: You may order a specific meal for each other Sim in the group. Use this interaction to order a date's favorite food for some extra Date score points.

◆ Order for All: Order the same dish for everyone in the group.

◆ Chef's Choice: Every Sim in the group orders his or her favorite food. Does not count for ordering a favorite food on a date and won't earn Date points.

**note**

If you wish to specify food for only some members of the party, order for those Sims by name, click on the Server, and select Done Ordering. The Server will bring the specified food as ordered and the favorite food of everyone else.

Especially if your Sim is on a date, it's a good idea to keep an eye on the date before ordering to see what his or her favorite food is. Once seated, he or she will flash a thought balloon of his or her favorite dish. Ordering a date's favorite food (rather than letting him or her do it) is a Date Event that can substantially improve Date score and make dining a fruitful dating activity. Because favorite foods are shown in pictures, it helps to know which represents which food:

Baked Alaska

Chili

Crepes

Filet Mignon

Fried Chicken

Hamburger

Layer Cake

Lime Seared Prawns

Lobster

Macaroni and Cheese

Nectarine Tartlette

Omelette

Pork Chops

Ribs

Salad

Salmon

Spaghetti and Meatballs

# GOING OUT: DATES, GROUPS, AND OUTINGS

Once everyone has finished their food, you can click on the Server to "Order." Group members may leave the table after the food is done but before the bill is paid; using Order again summons them back to the table.

## Cooking and Serving Food

Once ordering is complete, the Server promptly delivers the order to the NPC Chef. The Chef sets about preparing the meal (it takes the same amount of time no matter how much food is ordered) and the Server brings the finished tray back to the table.

## Eating Restaurant Food

When the food arrives at the table, Sims commence eating and conversing. Additionally, all table and/or booth socials are available while everyone is seated.

**note**
During a date, using the nested table socials (e.g., Caress Hand, Blow Kiss, etc.) are very important to improving Date score while eating.

Sure, eating at a restaurant is expensive, but you get both Hunger and Fun satisfaction. Generally, the more expensive the food, the more Hunger and Fun it delivers. Appetizers and desserts tend to offer less Hunger satisfaction but more Fun than a similarly priced entrée.

**note**
While eating, your Sim's needs deplete more slowly than normal.

## Dining Socials

Sims chatter incessantly among themselves, especially at the dinner table.

While seated at a dining table or counter, Sims can engage in several new socials and an expanded Talk interaction. Dining interactions are highlighted in their respective social menus by a chair-shaped icon:

◆ Table talk: whenever Sims dine together (either at home or out), they now talk and eat more realistically and interactively.

◆ Caress Hands: A Flirt romantic social that increases relationship. Sims must be seated adjacently.

◆ Feed a Bite: A Flirt romantic social that requires the initiating Sim to have food in front of him or her. Sims must be seated adjacently.

◆ Steal a Bite: A Play romantic social that requires the target Sim have food in front of him or her. Sims must be seated adjacently.

◆ Toast: An Entertain interaction, initiated by clicking on the Sim to be toasted.

◆ Throw Food: A Play interaction that provides Fun and reduces Hygiene.

◆ Throw Drink in Face: An Irritate interaction that decreases relationship. Can invoke the furious state if relationship is low enough. (see Chapter 9). Sims must be seated adjacently or across from each other.

◆ Blow Kiss: A Kiss romantic interaction that increases relationship. Sims must be seated adjacently.

◆ Surprise Engagement: A Propose interaction done while seated at the table. Can increase relationship and make Sims engaged but,

if rejected, will cause a massive loss of Date points and end the date with a Horrible score.

Booth socials let your Sims really let loose with the public displays of affection.

If Sims are eating in a booth, they also have access to booth-based interactions (Love Talk, and Hot Smooch). These having nothing to do with dining per se, but will increase a Date or Outing score. If your Sims are dining, Love Talk and Hot Smooch appear as interactions on the menu. If, however, they're merely sitting in a dining booth, the Sims must first Cuddle before these interactions become available.

## Dining Disasters

During a meal, two untoward things can happen:

Snoooooore! A very tired Sim could humiliate him- or herself by falling asleep at the table.

◆ Sim falls asleep: If, during a meal, a Sim's Energy drops too low, there's a random chance he or she can fall asleep in his plate. It's embarrassing and will, with most Sims, cause a sizeable reduction in Date or Outing score (particularly if the other Sim is Mean or a Popularity Sim and less of if he's Nice or a Family Sim).

◆ Waiter Drops Food: There is always a random chance the Server will drop a tray of food on your Sim. The better your relationship with the Server, the less likely this is to happen. Conversely, the worse your relationship is, the more often it'll occur. Getting food dumped on your Sim will seriously affect Date (though not Outing) score and any Mean Sims or children will applaud and laugh. How your Sim reacts depends on their Playful/Serious personality trait (Playful will laugh too. Serious will get angry). The lesson: be nice to your Servers or else! As for Date score, this mishap affects Sloppy and Popularity Sims the least and Neat and Fortune Sims the most.

## Finishing the Meal

When all Sims finish their food, the plates are cleared. At this point, the group will likely begin to leave the table. If you wish to continue dining, click on the Server and select "Order." This summons all group members back to the table and the Server comes to take another order.

If, on the other hand, you want to end the meal, you can pay for your meal...or not.

## Paying for a Meal

To pay for a meal, click on the Server, the Host, or the host podium and select Pay Bill. The amount of the bill will be deducted from your Sim's family funds.

Click on the Server, the Host, or the host podium to pay the bill.

If your Sim doesn't have enough money to cover the bill, her relationship with the Host and Server will be damaged (bad if you're trying to get a complimentary dinner in the future). This also severely reduces Date score. The cost of the meal will be added to your Sim's next delivery of household bills.

If you have a restaurant coupon in your inventory, you can use it for a bill of any amount at any restaurant in any neighborhood by choosing Use Coupon. The coupon is then removed from your Sim's inventory, the bill is paid, and no funds are deducted.

If you forget to settle up the bill and try to leave the lot, the Host delivers a stern lecture and the amount of the meal is deducted. Relationship with the Host and Server will be somewhat reduced and Date/Outing score will be slightly decreased.

## Skipping Out on Bill

Any time before the eating is complete, your Sim can skip out on the bill. If he or she can avoid capture for 45 seconds, he or she gets a free meal with no damage to relationship with the Host or Servers. Depending on the personality or Aspiration of your Sim's companions, there will be either a major increase or decrease in Date score (depending on whether your Sim's companion is Mean or Nice and whether he or she is a Fortune or a Family Sim).

Stay far away from the Host and you'll get away with it; he's very busy and has a very short memory.

To begin this scam, click on the host podium or the Host and select Skip Out on Bill.

 **tip**

For a head start, wait until the Host is on the telephone or seating a table before beginning the Skip Out on Bill. Because Hosts can't give chase until their conversation is over, you'll get some extra time.

Stay away from the Host until the on-screen timer runs out. If the Host gets within reach of your Sim (within three tiles) before time runs out, your Sim's nicked.

Busted Sims get a very stern lecture, a massive drop in Host/Server relationship, a possibly large fall in Date or Outing score, and an extra penalty added to the bill. Of course, he or she also has to pony up the amount of the tab.

## Chapter 6
# New Objects

The new goodies and furnishings introduced in *The Sims 2 Nightlife* are geared toward making every lot a hipper, more happenin' pad. Update your Sims' décor or add new fun activities that are just as at home in a Sim's living room as on a busy Community Lot.

This chapter includes all the details, obvious and hidden, about all these new objects and their interactions. Find general details and depreciation information in the Object Directory, and the nitty-gritties and pictures in the Object Catalog.

## Object Directory

| Object | Price | Initial Depreciation | Daily Depreciation | Depreciation Limit | Hunger | Comfort | Hygiene | Bladder | Energy | Fun | Environment | Cleaning | Study | Charisma | Creativity | Body | Logic | Mechanical | Cooking | Function | Kids | Study | Dining Room | Outside | Living Room | Bathroom | Bedroom | Kitchen | Miscellaneous | Street | Outdoor | Shopping | Food |
|---|---|---|---|---|---|---|---|---|---|---|---|---|---|---|---|---|---|---|---|---|---|---|---|---|---|---|---|---|---|---|---|---|---|
| '52 Pickup' Card Table | $650 | $95 | $65 | $252 | 0 | 0 | 0 | 0 | 0 | 0 | 0 | | | | | | | | | Surfaces | | | x | | x | | | | x | | | | |
| "A-Stroke" by Alfred D'Simms | $1,700 | $170 | $100 | $680 | 0 | 0 | 0 | 0 | 0 | 0 | 1 | | | | | | | | | Decorative | | x | | | x | | | | x | | | | |
| American tableau Table | $475 | $54 | $43 | $170 | 0 | 0 | 0 | 0 | 0 | 0 | 0 | | | | | | | | | Surfaces | | x | x | | x | | | | x | | | | |
| An Anonymous Masterpiece | $800 | $80 | $80 | $80 | 0 | 0 | 0 | 0 | 0 | 0 | 1 | | | | | | | | | Decorative | | x | | | x | | | | x | | | | |
| "B-Stroke" by Alfred D'Simno | $1,700 | $170 | $100 | $680 | 0 | 0 | 0 | 0 | 0 | 0 | 1 | | | | | | | | | Decorative | | x | | | x | | | | x | | | | |
| BeamElite Compacto Wall lamp by Rev-Siens | $200 | $28 | $25 | $64 | 0 | 0 | 0 | 0 | 0 | 0 | 0 | | | | | | | | | Lighting | | | | | | | x | | | | | | |
| BeamElite Extended Wall Lamp by Rev Client | $225 | $34 | $25 | $60 | 0 | 0 | 0 | 0 | 0 | 0 | 0 | | | | | | | | | Lighting | | | | | x | | x | | | | | | |
| Shablamm! Extended wall lamp by Frolic Lightning Design | $50 | $5 | $5 | $20 | 0 | 0 | 0 | 0 | 0 | 0 | 0 | | | | | | | | | Lighting | | x | | | | | | | | | | | |
| "Biggie is Better" Wall Mirror by ExPand | $450 | $45 | $58 | $232 | 0 | 0 | 0 | 0 | 0 | 0 | 3 | | | | | x | | | | Decorative | | x | | | x | | x | | x | | | | |
| Bit O'This and That | $150 | $22 | $15 | $60 | 0 | 0 | 0 | 0 | 0 | 0 | 0 | | | | | | | | | Decorative | | x | | | | | | | | | | | |
| Bust of Telqnda | $3,100 | $80 | $80 | $80 | 0 | 0 | 0 | 0 | 0 | 0 | 0 | | | | | | | | | Decorative | | | | | | | | | | | | | |
| "C-Stroke" by Alfred D'Simno | $1,700 | $170 | $100 | $680 | 0 | 0 | 0 | 0 | 0 | 0 | 1 | | | | | | | | | Decorative | | x | | | x | | | | x | | | | |
| Cantankerous Splinters | $2,750 | $305 | $105 | $1,400 | 0 | 7 | 0 | 0 | 4 | 0 | 0 | | | | | | | | | Comfort | | | | | x | | | | x | | | | |
| "Cantenergy Counter" by Wood Kou Stalexc Formashings | $1,880 | $102 | $168 | $900 | 0 | 0 | 0 | 0 | 0 | 0 | 0 | | | | | | | | | Surfaces | | | | | | | | x | x | | | | x |
| Chinzz fanssed Incandescent Flush File | $30 | $15 | $3 | $12 | 0 | 0 | 0 | 0 | 0 | 0 | 2 | | | | | | | | | Surfaces | | x | | | x | | | | x | | | x | |
| Dedmar "Flayrd" All purpose Counter | $750 | $85 | $75 | $300 | 0 | 0 | 0 | 0 | 0 | 0 | 0 | | | | | | | | | Surfaces | | | | | | | | x | x | | | | x |
| Children Safety Sign | $700 | $85 | $65 | $245 | 0 | 0 | 0 | 0 | 0 | 5 | 0 | | x | | x | | | | | Electronica | x | x | x | | | | | | x | | | x | |
| ClubiCube by Lumnissement Projections | $5 | $0 | $0 | $0 | 0 | 0 | 0 | 0 | 0 | 3 | 0 | | | | | | | | | Decorative | | | | | x | | | | x | | | | x |
| "Compulsion" Fregrance Display | $3,500 | $395 | $350 | $1,400 | 0 | 0 | 0 | 0 | 0 | 0 | 0 | | | | | | | | | Miscellaneous | | x | | | | | | | x | | | x | |
| "Contempo" Dining Chair by Ernesto Delarosso | $650 | $78 | $35 | $340 | 0 | 2 | 0 | 0 | 0 | 0 | 0 | | | | | | | | | Comfort | x | x | x | | x | | | x | x | | | | |
| Dancing Friend Jukebox | $650 | $65 | $40 | $440 | 0 | 0 | 0 | 0 | 0 | 7 | 0 | | | | | | | | | Electronica | | x | | | x | | | | x | | | | |
| Deep Sleeper by Igor and Sans | $1,300 | $65 | $150 | $900 | 0 | 9 | 0 | 0 | 9 | 0 | 0 | | | | | | | | | Comfort | | | | | | | x | | x | | | | |
| "Fluorescents Forswear" Wall Light | $500 | $75 | $50 | $200 | 0 | 0 | 0 | 0 | 0 | 0 | 2 | | | | | | | | | Lighting | | | | | | | | | x | x | | x | x |
| Electroliiance Sphere by Limitliness Unlimited | $3,500 | $525 | $350 | $1,400 | 0 | 0 | 0 | 0 | 0 | 10 | 0 | | | | | | | | | Hobbies | | | | x | | | | | x | | | x | |
| EverGlow "Maximum Red | $975 | $98 | $68 | $878 | 0 | 0 | 0 | 0 | 0 | 0 | 0 | | | | | | | | | Lighting | | | x | | | | | | x | | | x | |
| EverGlow "Maximum Red | $975 | $97 | $68 | $878 | 0 | 0 | 0 | 0 | 0 | 0 | 0 | | | | | | | | | Lighting | | | x | | | | | | x | | | x | |
| EverGlow Uranium Rod | $970 | $26 | $17 | $58 | 0 | 0 | 0 | 0 | 0 | 0 | 0 | | | | | | | | | Lighting | | x | | | | | | | x | | | x | |
| Exclaim! Sign | $75 | $8 | $0 | $0 | 0 | 0 | 0 | 0 | 0 | 0 | 0 | | | | | | | | | Hobbies | | | | | | | | | x | | | | x |
| Fat City Counters | $650 | $65 | $53 | $252 | 0 | 0 | 0 | 0 | 0 | 0 | 0 | | | | | | | | | Surfaces | | x | x | | | | | x | x | | | | x |

The Sims 2 Nightlife — EXPANSION PACK

| Object | Price | Price | Price | | | | | | | | Category |
|---|---|---|---|---|---|---|---|---|---|---|---|
| Neon Flamingo | $225 | $54 | $81 | 0 | 0 | 0 | 0 | 0 | 0 | | Lighting |
| "Macallan" by Maestro | $2,100 | $277 | $185 | 0 | 0 | 0 | 0 | 0 | 0 | | Miscellaneous |
| "Wunderwall" by Aeterna | $330 | $99 | $74 | 0 | 0 | 0 | 0 | 0 | 0 | | Surfaces |
| Medium Art by "Hera" | $400 | $59 | $236 | 0 | 0 | 0 | 0 | 0 | 0 | | Electronics |
| Stir Rock Wall Speaker | $400 | $40 | $80 | 0 | 0 | 0 | 0 | 0 | 0 | | Electronics |
| Medium Speakers "Iso/Helion" | $400 | $40 | $80 | 0 | 0 | 0 | 0 | 0 | 0 | | Electronics |
| Baltazar Wall Speaker | $900 | $40 | $450 | 0 | 0 | 0 | 0 | 0 | 0 | | Electronics |
| One Pin, Two Pin | $225 | $19 | $50 | 0 | 0 | 0 | 0 | 0 | 2 | | Hobbies |
| Perfect Pennant | $850 | $22 | $80 | 0 | 0 | 0 | 0 | 0 | 12 | | Decorative |
| "Pineapple" by Lynn O'Steve | $80 | $13 | $80 | 0 | 0 | 0 | 0 | 0 | 10 | | Lighting |
| "Phunster 300" Bowling Alley by Hurling Fun Products, Inc. | $5,500 | $550 | $2,100 | 0 | 0 | 0 | 5 | 0 | 1 | | |
| Potted Ficus | $800 | $48 | $228 | 0 | 0 | 0 | 0 | 0 | 0 | | Decorative |
| Rented Palm | $320 | $52 | $240 | 0 | 0 | 0 | 0 | 0 | 3 | | Decorative |
| "Tented Plant in Spiral..." | $85 | $25 | $85 | 0 | 0 | 0 | 0 | 0 | 0 | | Decorative |
| Elegance, an existential piece by Natural Pretzel | $510 | $98 | $510 | 0 | 0 | 0 | 0 | 0 | 0 | | Decorative |
| Potted Potential | $300 | $90 | $90 | 0 | 0 | 0 | 0 | 0 | 0 | | Decorative |
| Rackmaster 550 Bowling Ball | $500 | $75 | $101 | 0 | 0 | 0 | 0 | 7 | 0 | | Decorative |
| Reach by Hurling Matters | $1,000 | $150 | $203 | 0 | 0 | 0 | 0 | 0 | 0 | | Decorative |
| Recalling Rug 3x3 | $990 | $101 | $403 | 0 | 0 | 0 | 0 | 0 | 0 | | Decorative |
| Recherché Counter-Island | $325 | $49 | $272 | 0 | 0 | 0 | 0 | 0 | 0 | | Decorative |
| Recherché Floor Runner | $850 | $85 | $80 | 0 | 0 | 0 | 0 | 0 | 0 | | Decorative |
| RakVeRecourt 109 | $2,750 | $275 | $580 | 0 | 0 | 0 | 0 | 0 | 0 | | Appliances Rewards |
| Ragnit Serial #5-CUPUA | $280 | $90 | $90 | 0 | 0 | 0 | 0 | 0 | 0 | | Decorative |
| Romantic Romance by Uptownus Vagrus | $900 | $90 | $90 | 0 | 0 | 0 | 0 | 0 | 0 | | Decorative |
| Noire 66 | $900 | $90 | $940 | 0 | 0 | 0 | 0 | 0 | 0 | | Decorative |
| Elle and Loy | $100 | $15 | $90 | 0 | 0 | 0 | 0 | 2 | 0 | | Lighting |
| "Sent to My Room Without Dinner" by Picca Ellie | $900 | $90 | $90 | 0 | 0 | 0 | 0 | 0 | 0 | | Decorative |
| Bludgman Kitchen Sink | $300 | $45 | $90 | 0 | 0 | 0 | 0 | 0 | 0 | | Plumbing |
| Signs of Elliptical Joy by Alexandra Workman | $100 | $15 | $90 | 0 | 0 | 0 | 0 | 0 | 0 | | Decorative |
| "Sims Want Walls Hoods" Sign/Burn Commercial Imagery | $70 | $50 | $50 | | | | | | | | Miscellaneous |
| "3x 'n'Brrr" Photo Booth from... | $1,300 | $55 | $740 | 0 | 0 | 0 | 0 | 0 | 0 | | Decorative |
| "Smoke" Sensed by Simpleson | $900 | $99 | $90 | 0 | 0 | 0 | 0 | 0 | 0 | | Comfort |
| Spring Majesty | $279 | $97 | $240 | 5 | 0 | 0 | 0 | 0 | 0 | | Lighting |
| "Squintessa" Vanity table lamp by Simoleon & Co. | $80 | $80 | $80 | 0 | 0 | 0 | 0 | 0 | 2 | | Decorative |
| Sway-Flre Sunburst | $80 | $37 | $44 | 0 | 0 | 0 | 0 | 0 | 0 | | Electronics |
| Sway-Flre Sunburst | $80 | $80 | $80 | 0 | 0 | 0 | 9 | 0 | 0 | | Electronics |
| Standard/Go 27" Widescreen TV | $600 | $220 | $370 | 0 | 0 | 0 | 0 | 0 | 0 | | Appliances |
| Stereomix 27" Multinod | $750 | $375 | $250 | 0 | 0 | 0 | 0 | 0 | 0 | | |
| V Television | $2,500 | $12,500 | $1,058 | 0 | 0 | 0 | 0 | 0 | 0 | | |
| Tempest Cooktop from Cuea | | | | | | | | | | | |

## Object Directory

| Object | Price | Initial Depreciation | Daily Depreciation | Depreciation Limit | Hunger | Comfort | Hygiene | Bladder | Energy | Fun | Environment | Cleaning | Study | Charisma | Creativity | Body | Logic | Mechanical | Cooking | Function | Kids | Study | Dining Room | Outside | Living Room | Bathroom | Bedroom | Kitchen | Miscellaneous | Street | Outdoor | Shopping | Food |
|---|---|---|---|---|---|---|---|---|---|---|---|---|---|---|---|---|---|---|---|---|---|---|---|---|---|---|---|---|---|---|---|---|---|
| Feckless Accessories for the Kitchen | $970 | $0 | $0 | $0 | 0 | 0 | 0 | 0 | 0 | 0 | 2 | | | | | | | | | Decorative | | | | | | | | × | | | | | × |
| "Starshine" Wall Light | $330 | $0 | $0 | $0 | 0 | 0 | 0 | 0 | 0 | 0 | 0 | | | | | | | | | Lighting | | | × | | × | | × | | | | | | |
| Frosted Font | $5,800 | $525 | $63 | $4,042 | 0 | 0 | 0 | 0 | 0 | 0 | 3 | | | | | | | | | Decorative | | | | × | | | | | | | × | | |
| Four Nougatines in repose | $325 | $35 | $5 | $225 | 0 | 0 | 0 | 0 | 0 | 0 | 0 | | | | | | | | | Decorative | | | | | × | | | | | | | | × |
| "Gastronomique" Restaurant Podium | $200 | $30 | $20 | $80 | 0 | 0 | 0 | 0 | 0 | 0 | 1 | | | | | | | | | Miscellaneous | | | | | | | | | × | | | | × |
| Real Taste Dining Table | $400 | $60 | $40 | $160 | 0 | 0 | 0 | 0 | 0 | 0 | 1 | | | | | | | | | Surfaces | | | × | | | | | × | | | | | × |
| Great Taste Dining Table | $610 | $91 | $61 | $244 | 0 | 0 | 0 | 0 | 0 | 0 | 1 | | | | | | | | | Surfaces | | | × | | | | | × | | | | | × |
| "Grilled Cheese" by Rena Renault | $10 | $0 | $0 | $0 | 0 | 0 | 0 | 0 | 0 | 0 | 1 | | | | | | | | | Decorative | | | | | × | | | | | | | | × |
| Hanging Flower by Cogun Ceramics | $10 | $0 | $0 | $0 | 0 | 0 | 0 | 0 | 0 | 0 | 2 | | | | | | | | | Decorative | | | | | × | | × | | | | | | × |
| Hestons Ristorante by Big Geeks | $340 | $51 | $34 | $136 | 0 | 0 | 0 | 0 | 0 | 0 | 2 | | | | | | | | | Decorative | | | | | × | | | | | | | | × |
| High Quail Metal Chair by Big Daz | $350 | $53 | $35 | $140 | 0 | 8 | 0 | 0 | 0 | 0 | 2 | | | | | | | | | Comfort | | | × | | × | | | | | | | | × |
| Hipster Mosaic in Pink | $950 | $27 | $15 | $190 | 0 | 0 | 0 | 0 | 0 | 0 | 2 | | | | | | | | | Decorative | | | | | × | | | | | | | | × |
| Hunka 7H by Hwang Matsura | $1,050 | $1,793 | $1,195 | $4,780 | 0 | 0 | 0 | 0 | 0 | 0 | 1 | | | | | | | | | Surfaces | | | | | × | | | | | | | | × |
| Impeccable Taste Dining Table | $850 | $128 | $85 | $340 | 0 | 0 | 0 | 0 | 0 | 0 | 1 | | | | | | | | | Surfaces | | | × | | | | | × | | | | | × |
| Jancutter's "Last Stand" Sectional Booth | $240 | $45 | $30 | $120 | 4 | 5 | 0 | 0 | 0 | 2 | 2 | | | | | | | | | Comfort | | | × | | × | | | | | | | | × |
| Juice On The Wall Sculpture | $300 | $0 | $0 | $0 | 0 | 0 | 0 | 0 | 0 | 0 | 0 | | | | | | | | | Decorative | | | | | × | | | | | | | | × |
| "La Table" Long Dining Table | $240 | $36 | $24 | $96 | 0 | 0 | 0 | 0 | 0 | 0 | 3 | | | | | | | | | Surfaces | | | × | | | | | × | | | | | × |
| "La Voile" Square Dining Table | $710 | $107 | $71 | $284 | 0 | 0 | 0 | 0 | 0 | 0 | 3 | | | | | | | | | Surfaces | | | × | | | | | × | | | | | × |
| Large Flower Arrangement | $825 | $124 | $16 | $82 | 0 | 0 | 0 | 0 | 0 | 0 | 2 | | | | | | | | | Decorative | | | × | | × | × | × | | | | | | × |
| "Lily Pads" by Max Pia | $770 | $0 | $0 | $0 | 0 | 0 | 0 | 0 | 0 | 0 | 1 | | | | | | | | | Decorative | | | | | × | × | × | | | | | | × |
| Llama Xing Sign | $85 | $14 | $0 | $0 | 0 | 0 | 0 | 0 | 0 | 0 | 1 | | | | | | | | | Decorative | × | | | × | | | | | | | × | | × |
| Lovetech Light Disc | $810 | $0 | $0 | $0 | 0 | 0 | 0 | 0 | 0 | 0 | 1 | | | | | | | | | Lighting | | × | | | × | | | | | | | | × |
| Marketing Print by Seph Epia | $330 | $0 | $0 | $0 | 0 | 0 | 0 | 0 | 0 | 0 | 2 | | | | | | | | | Decorative | | × | | | × | | × | | | | | | × |
| Modart Nouleau Mirror (3-panel) | $680 | $0 | $0 | $0 | 0 | 0 | 0 | 0 | 0 | 0 | 2 | × | × | | | | | | | Decorative | | × | | | × | × | × | | | | | | × |
| Modart Nouleau Mirror (9-panel) | $650 | $97 | $58 | $232 | 0 | 0 | 0 | 0 | 0 | 0 | 2 | × | × | | | | | | | Decorative | | × | | | × | × | × | | | | | | × |
| Molded Sectional "Marre Sheela" Dining Chair by WardMeld | $650 | $97 | $65 | $232 | 0 | 0 | 0 | 0 | 0 | 0 | 3 | | | | | | | | | Comfort | | | × | | | | | | | | | | × |
| Miss Simplistica | $650 | $23 | $15 | $260 | 0 | 6 | 0 | 0 | 0 | 0 | 3 | | | | | | | | | Comfort | × | | × | | × | | × | | | | | | × |
| "Mr. Sensitive" by Comfortloude | $255 | $38 | $25 | $102 | 0 | 8 | 0 | 0 | 0 | 0 | 1 | | | | | | | | | Comfort | | | | | × | | | | | | | | × |
| "Mr. Sensitive with Arms" by Comfortloude | $280 | $39 | $26 | $104 | 0 | 8 | 0 | 0 | 0 | 0 | 1 | | | | | | | | | Comfort | | | | | × | | × | | | | | | × |
| "Nature's Perfection" by E.Z. Phun | $289 | $0 | $0 | $0 | 0 | 0 | 0 | 0 | 0 | 0 | 2 | | | | | | | | | Decorative | × | | | | × | | × | | | | | | × |

# Object Directory

| Object | Price | Initial Depreciation | Daily Depreciation | Depreciation Limit | Hunger | Comfort | Hygiene | Bladder | Energy | Fun | Environment | Cleaning | Study | Charisma | Creativity | Body | Logic | Mechanical | Cooking | Function | Kids | Study | Dining Room | Outside | Living Room | Bathroom | Bedroom | Kitchen | Miscellaneous | Street | Outdoor | Shopping | Food |
|---|---|---|---|---|---|---|---|---|---|---|---|---|---|---|---|---|---|---|---|---|---|---|---|---|---|---|---|---|---|---|---|---|---|
| "That Place Over There" by Native Blur | $550 | $83 | $83 | $83 | 0 | 0 | 0 | 0 | 0 | 0 | 1 | | | | | | | | | Decorative | | | | | | | | | x | | | | |
| The "Sometimes A Man is An Island" Counter Island by Neantha | $530 | $53 | $80 | $80 | 0 | 0 | 0 | 0 | 0 | 0 | 0 | | | | | | | | | Surfaces | | | x | | | | | x | | | | | |
| The Forbidden Fruit Counter by Neantha | $590 | $59 | $59 | $236 | 0 | 0 | 0 | 0 | 0 | 0 | 0 | | | | | | | | | Surfaces | | | x | | | | | x | | | | | |
| Her Fun Spot Kids Rug | $425 | $64 | $64 | $170 | 0 | 0 | 0 | 0 | 0 | 2 | 0 | | | | | | | | | Decorative | x | | | | x | | x | | | | | | |
| The Bobo-a-Go-Go | $255 | $29 | $43 | $102 | 0 | 0 | 0 | 0 | 0 | 0 | 0 | | | | | | | | | Decorative | | | | | x | | x | | | | | | |
| Spotlight by LumiD | $425 | $64 | $64 | $170 | 0 | 0 | 0 | 0 | 0 | 0 | 0 | | | | | | | | | Lighting | | | | | x | | | | x | | | | |
| Itsy Gray Woman of SimCity | $180,000 | $0 | $0 | $0 | 0 | 0 | 0 | 0 | 0 | 0 | 2 | | | | | | | | | Decorative | | | | | | | | | x | | | | |
| "The Grease Stands Alone" Island Bar | $1,780 | $277 | $740 | $740 | 0 | 0 | 0 | 0 | 0 | 0 | 3 | | | | | | | | | Miscellaneous | | | | x | x | | | x | | | | x | x |
| Portal Player 8000 Professional DJ Booth by HartBeats | $2,750 | $413 | $1,025 | $1,100 | 0 | 0 | 0 | 0 | 0 | 2 | 0 | | | | x | | | | | Miscellaneous | | | | | x | | | | x | | | | |
| The HartCorp Burning B-R Series Fire a-Jar | $325 | $33 | $33 | $130 | 0 | 0 | 0 | 0 | 0 | 0 | 1 | | | | | | | | | Decorative | | | | | x | | | | x | | | | |
| BSK Heated Metalchism | $875 | $88 | $88 | $350 | 0 | 0 | 0 | 0 | 0 | 0 | 2 | | | | | | | | | Miscellaneous | | | | | x | | | | x | | | | |
| The LandiceKnife by Havenida | $4,250 | $538 | $425 | $1,700 | 0 | 4 | 0 | 0 | 0 | 0 | 1 | | | | | | | | | Miscellaneous | | | | | | | | | x | | | | |
| The Glaani | $1,650 | $277 | $665 | $740 | 0 | 0 | 0 | 0 | 0 | 0 | 2 | | | | | | | | | Decorative | | | x | | x | | | | | | | | |
| The "Sompson" HandBat by SuperSimCorp | $340 | $15 | $15 | $40 | 0 | 0 | 0 | 0 | 0 | 2 | 0 | | | | | | | | | Electronics | | | | | x | | x | | | | | | |
| The Phono HandBat by LumiD | $375 | $54 | $54 | $279 | 0 | 0 | 0 | 0 | 0 | 2 | 0 | | | | | | | | | Electronics | | | | | x | | x | | | | | | |
| The Qube | $550 | $53 | $106 | $106 | — | 0 | 0 | 0 | 2 | 0 | 0 | | | | | | | | | Surfaces | | | | | x | | | | x | | | | |
| The Shadow Streamer | $550 | $53 | $53 | $280 | 0 | 0 | 0 | 0 | 2 | 0 | 0 | | | | | | | | | Lighting | | | | | x | | | | x | | | | |
| The Smooge Minima | $43 | $43 | $35 | $80 | 0 | 0 | 0 | 0 | 0 | 0 | 0 | | | | | | | | | Lighting | | | | | x | | | | x | | | | |
| Blis Sound' FX228 | $2,250 | $338 | $725 | $900 | 0 | 0 | 0 | 0 | 0 | 0 | 0 | | | | | | | | | Decorative | | | | | | | | | x | | | x | x |
| The Surrewald Scene | $430 | $0 | $0 | $0 | 0 | 0 | 0 | 0 | 0 | 0 | 0 | | | | | | | | | Comfort | | | | | x | | | | | | | | |
| The Sumpsung Breaseray Breatbat | $690 | $102 | $198 | $277 | 0 | 0 | 0 | 0 | 0 | 0 | 0 | | | | | | | | | Decorative | | | | x | x | | | x | | | | | |
| The Yamuhotta Evasion | $18,250 | $538 | $625 | $2,500 | 0 | 0 | 0 | 0 | 0 | 6 | 0 | | | | | | | | | Miscellaneous | | | | | x | | | | x | | | | |
| Sharay' the herb star "Two Dogs and an Olive" by Maxi Rugg | $850 | $85 | $85 | $340 | 0 | 5 | 0 | 0 | 0 | 0 | 0 | | | | | | | | | Decorative | | x | x | | x | | x | | x | | | | x |
| Glass-Slugar Deluxe Curves | $12,990 | $0 | $0 | $0 | 0 | 0 | 0 | 0 | 0 | 2 | 2 | | | | x | | | | | Decorative | | | | x | x | | | | x | | | | |
| "Unbridled Barolk' Dwé Rug | $77 | $80 | $80 | $80 | 0 | 0 | 0 | 0 | 0 | 0 | 0 | | | | | | | | | Decorative | | | | | x | | | | x | | | | |
| Vintage Kerro Gamé | $350 | $53 | $35 | $40 | 0 | 0 | 0 | 0 | 0 | 4 | 0 | | | | | | | | | Electronics | | x | x | | x | | | x | x | | x | | x |
| Dining table | $235 | $35 | $24 | $102 | 0 | 0 | 0 | 0 | 0 | 0 | 0 | | | | | | | | | Surfaces | | x | x | | | | | x | | | x | | x |
| "Marvai" Dining Table | $9,500 | $75 | $152 | $200 | 0 | 0 | 0 | 0 | 0 | 0 | 0 | | | | | | | | | Surfaces | | | x | | | | | x | | | | | x |
| Vintage Kerro Gamé Machine | $1,600 | $220 | $182 | $720 | 0 | 0 | 0 | 0 | 0 | 8 | 4 | | | | | | | | | Electronics | | x | | x | x | | | | x | | x | | x |

# Object Catalog

## Comfort

### Dining Chairs

**Jacuster's "Last Stand" Sectional Booth**
◆ Price: $300
◆ Need Effects: Comfort 8, Energy 2 (Nap)

Though you could use individual Jacusters as dining chairs, they're designed to do much more. They're actually the components of a restaurant-grade, intelligently connecting booth bench.

Place pieces next to each other and they link to form a continuous bench. Turn a piece at a right angle to an existing piece and it'll form a corner. Arrange these pieces with either exterior or interior corners.

There are a few limitations to what your Sims can do on a booth bench. They can't sit on the corner segments. Sims must sit adjacent to each other to perform any of the exclusively booth-based Cuddle interactions.

**note**
If Sims are sitting so as to block access to parts of a booth bench (i.e. two Sims at either booth opening with several seats around the corner between them), don't fret. Other Sims can magically "leapfrog" into those obstructed seats.

**note**
All booth interactions are marked with the gold dining chair icon.

Interactions:

◆ Cuddle: Sims snuggle close for a little romance but must be sitting next to each other. Your Sims must be cuddling to do the other romantic booth socials.

◆ Love Talk: While cuddling, Sims whisper sweet nothings.

◆ Hot Smooch: Sims canoodle freely in the booth.

**note**
Connecting booth benches will connect with other pieces of the same kind regardless of their color or design. Thus, each part of the bench can be a different color as long as all pieces are the same object.

**Hipster Metal Chair by Big Daddy**
◆ Price: $350
◆ Need Effects: Comfort 4, Environment 1

**"More Sleeka" Dining Chair by Simplonics**
◆ Price: $650
◆ Need Effects: Comfort 6, Environment 1

**"Contorto" Dining Chair by Ernesto Doloroso**
◆ Price: $850
◆ Need Effects: Comfort 7, Environment 2

### Sofas and Loveseats

**Molded Sectional by WorldMold**
◆ Price: $150
◆ Need Effects: Comfort 6 (Sit), Comfort 5 (Lounge), Energy 1 (Nap), Fun 4 (Play)
◆ Need Max: Energy up to 20 (Nap)

Unlike Jacuster's "Last Stand" Sectional Booth, these intelligently connecting booths can't be used as dining chairs and won't offer the special booth-based Cuddle interactions (Hot Smooch and Love Talk).

However, that doesn't decrease their utility or their utter coolness. They're just really flexible and smart connecting sofas.

## "Mr. Section" by Comfortitude

- ◆ Price: §255
- ◆ Need Effects: Comfort 8 (Sit), Comfort 5 (Lounge), Energy 2 (Nap), Fun 4 (Play)
- ◆ Need Max: Energy up to 20 (Nap)

See Molded Sectional by WorldMold, above.

Mr. Section and Mr. Section with Arms can be interconnected. If an armed piece is has pieces on both sides, it automatically converts to an unarmed Mr. Section piece.

## "Mr. Section with Arms" by Comfortitude

- ◆ Price: §260
- ◆ Need Effects: Comfort 8 (Sit), Comfort 5 (Lounge), Energy 2 (Nap), Fun 4 (Play)
- ◆ Need Max: Energy up to 20 (Nap)

See Molded Sectional by WorldMold, above.

Mr. Section and Mr. Section with arms can be interconnected. If an armed piece is has pieces on both sides, it automatically converts to an unarmed Mr. Section piece.

## Beds
### Deep Sleeper by Igor and Sons

- ◆ Price: §1,500
- ◆ Need Effects: Comfort 1, Energy 7, Comfort -2 (Scared), Comfort -1 (Creeped), Fun 2 (Dare to Peek)

 **note**

With all other beds, when a sleeping Sim's Energy is fully restored, he or she will autonomously wake up. The coffin behaves differently when a vampire sleeps in it. Even after the vampire's Energy is restored, he or she won't awaken autonomously unless (and until) it's dark outside. At sunset, a vampire will autonomously awaken and exit the coffin unless Energy is not yet fully restored. Once the sun sets, the vampire will arise autonomously when fully rested.

Interactions:

- ◆ Sleep: Non-vampire Sims can sleep in the coffin as a regular bed. Vampire Sims sleep in the coffin with a special spooky animation. While vampires are in the coffin, all Need decay freezes.
- ◆ Wake Up: Non-vampire Sim sleeping in coffin will rise just as from normal bed.
- ◆ Arise: Vampire will wake from sleep and get out of coffin regardless of time of day.
- ◆ Peek: If a vampire is sleeping in the coffin, another Sim can peek inside. As a result, the peeking Sim will be either creeped out and close the lid or the vampire will frighten the Sim before returning to sleep. Both cause a loss of Comfort, but being frightened is more severe and causes all the usual possible fright responses: run away, bladder failure, and, (in rare instances when a Sim's Needs are very low) scared to death. If the peeking Sim is a vampire, he or she will always just be creeped out. Visitors will peek autonomously but playable Sims never will.

◆ Dare to Peek: A Sim can dare a second Sim to peek in the coffin. If the dared Sim is creeped out, both Sims get Fun. If the peeking Sim's bladder fails, the daring Sim gets lots of Fun and the dared Sim gets a bit to go with his or her loss of Hygiene. If the peeking Sim is scared to death, the daring Sim gets no Fun. See Chapter 7 for details on availability, acceptance, and relationship and social results.

## Miscellaneous

**Hipster Barstool by Big Daddy**
◆ Price: $340
◆ Need Effects: Comfort 5

**"Sleeka" Barstool by Simplonics**
◆ Price: $600
◆ Need Effects: Comfort 5, Environment 1

**The Sumptuous Brasserie Barstool**
◆ Price: $680
◆ Need Effects: Comfort 6, Environment 1

## Surfaces

### Counters

All kitchen island counters, old and new, now can intelligently turn corners. Note that islands can make interior corners only, not exterior, and they won't connect with normal counters. They will,

however, connect with matching island bars (found in the Miscellaneous/Party catalog).

**The Forbidden Fruit Counter by Neontrix**
◆ Price: $590

**"NeonServe" by Neontrix**
◆ Price: $590

**Fat City Counters**
◆ Price: $630

**The "Sometimes A Man Is An Island" Counter Island, by Fat City Counters**
◆ Price: $630

**"Castanoga" Counter by Wood You Believe Furnishings**
◆ Price: $680

**"La Table" Square Dining Table**
- Price: $710
- Need Effects: Environment 1

**Recherché Counter Island**
- Price: $680

## Tables

**Vintage Retro Classic Dining Table**
- Price: $235

**Good Taste Dining Table**
- Price: $400

**American Tableau Table**
- Price: $425

**"Visivue" Dining Table**
- Price: $500

**Great Taste Dining Table**
- Price: $810
- Need Effects: Environment 2

**Impeccable Taste Dining Table**
- Price: $850
- Need Effects: Environment 2

**"La Table" Long Dining Table**
- Price: $876
- Need Effect: Environment 2

## Coffee Tables

**The Qube**
- Price: $340

## Decorative

### Plants

**Hanging Flower by Copur Ceramics**
- ◆ Price: $100
- ◆ Need Effects: Environment 1

**Large Flower Arrangement**
- ◆ Price: $155
- ◆ Need Effects: Environment 1

**Potted Ficus from Nature's Garden**
- ◆ Price: $320
- ◆ Need Effects: Environment 2

**"Potted Plant in Spiral Elegance," an existential piece by Natural Pretzel**
- ◆ Price: $510
- ◆ Need Effects: Environment 3

**Potted Palm**
- ◆ Price: $600
- ◆ Need Effects: Environment 3

## Sculptures

**Bit O'This and That**
- ◆ Price: $150
- ◆ Need Effects: Fun 3 (View), Environment 1
- ◆ Need Max: Fun up to 95 (View)

**Potted Potential**
- ◆ Price: $300
- ◆ Need Effects: Fun 3 (View), Environment 2
- ◆ Need Max: Fun up to 95 (View)

**The Sorrowful Scions**
- ◆ Price: $450
- ◆ Need Effects: Fun 3 (View), Environment 4
- ◆ Need Max: Fun up to 95 (View)

**Rackmaster 850 Bowling Ball Rack by Hurling Matters**
- ◆ Price: $2,000
- ◆ Need Effects: Fun 3 (View), Environment 10
- ◆ Need Max: Fun up to 95 (View)

**note**
This object is purely decorative and isn't required for a bowling alley to function.

**Bust of Tylopoda**
- ◆ Price: $3,130
- ◆ Need Effects: Fun 3 (View), Environment 10
- ◆ Need Max: Fun up to 95 (View)

![The Sims 2 Nightlife Expansion Pack]

### Florid Font

◆ Price: $5,800

◆ Need Effects: Fun 3 (View), Environment 10

◆ Need Max: Fun up to 95 (View)

**Interactions:**

◆ Add Soap: Sim adds detergent to fountain to make it sudsy.

### The Gray Woman of SimCity

◆ Price: $6,000

◆ Need Effects: Fun 3 (View), Environment 10

◆ Need Max: Fun up to 95 (View)

## Wall Hangings

### Feckless Accessories for the Kitchen

◆ Price: $70

◆ Need Effects: Fun 3 (View), Environment 1

◆ Need Max: Fun up to 95 (View)

### "Sims Must Wash Hands" Sign

◆ Price: $70

◆ Need Effects: Fun 3 (View), Environment 1

◆ Need Max: Fun up to 95 (View)

### Llama Xing Sign

◆ Price: $70

◆ Need Effects: Fun 3 (View), Environment 1

◆ Need Max: Fun up to 95 (View)

### Children Safety Sign

◆ Price: $70

◆ Need Effects: Fun 3 (View), Environment 1

◆ Need Max: Fun up to 95 (View)

### Exclaim! Sign

◆ Price: $71

◆ Need Effects: Fun 3 (View), Environment 1

◆ Need Max: Fun up to 95 (View)

### Uber-Duper Deluxe Curves Ahead Sign

◆ Price: $72

◆ Need Effects: Fun 3 (View), Environment 1

◆ Need Max: Fun up to 95 (View)

### An Anonymous Masterpiece

◆ Price: $110

◆ Need Effects: Fun 3 (View), Environment 1

◆ Need Max: Fun up to 95 (View)

### Reprint Serial #S-COPU4

◆ Price: $130

◆ Need Effects: Fun 3 (View), Environment 1

◆ Need Max: Fun up to 95 (View)

### Route 66
◆ Price: $200
◆ Need Effects: Fun 3 (View), Environment 2
◆ Need Max: Fun up to 95 (View)

### Spring Majesty
◆ Price: $291
◆ Need Effects: Fun 3 (View), Environment 2
◆ Need Max: Fun up to 95 (View)

### "Nature's Perfection" by E.Z. Phun
◆ Price: $299
◆ Need Effects: Fun 3 (View), Environment 2
◆ Need Max: Fun up to 95 (View)

### Four Vegetables in repose
◆ Price: $325
◆ Need Effects: Fun 3 (View), Environment 3
◆ Need Max: Fun up to 95 (View)

### Marketing Print by Seph Epia
◆ Price: $330
◆ Need Effects: Fun 3 (View), Environment 3
◆ Need Max: Fun up to 95 (View)

### "That Place Over There" by Retina Bluri
◆ Price: $550
◆ Need Effects: Fun 3 (View), Environment 4
◆ Need Max: Fun up to 95 (View)

### "Lily Pads" by Myo Pia
◆ Price: $625
◆ Need Effects: Fun 3 (View), Environment 5
◆ Need Max: Fun up to 95 (View)

### "Pineapple" by Lynn D'Saye
◆ Price: $850
◆ Need Effects: Fun 3 (View), Environment 6
◆ Need Max: Fun up to 95 (View)

### "Grilled Cheese" by Renu Tumush
◆ Price: $850
◆ Need Effects: Fun 3 (View), Environment 6
◆ Need Max: Fun up to 95 (View)

### "Sent to My Room Without Dinner" by Picts Ellie
◆ Price: $900
◆ Need Effects: Fun 3 (View), Environment 6
◆ Need Max: Fun up to 95 (View)

### "A Stroke" by Alfred D'Simvo
- Price: $1,700
- Need Effects: Fun 3 (View), Environment 10
- Need Max: Fun up to 95 (View)

### "B Stroke" by Alfred D'Simvo
- Price: $1,700
- Need Effects: Fun 3 (View), Environment 10
- Need Max: Fun up to 95 (View)

### "C Stroke" by Alfred D'Simvo
- Price: $1,700
- Need Effects: Fun 3 (View), Environment 10
- Need Max: Fun up to 95 (View)

### Cantankerous Splatters
- Price: $2,750
- Need Effects: Fun 3 (View), Environment 10
- Need Max: Fun up to 95 (View)

### "Two Dogs and an Olive" by Mixt Hupp
- Price: $2,900
- Need Effects: Fun 3 (View), Environment 10
- Need Max: Fun up to 95 (View)

## Mirrors

### "Bigger is Better" Wall Mirror by ExPand
- Price: $450
- Skill: Charisma (Practice Romance or Practice Speech)
- Need Effects: Hygiene 2 (Gussy Up), Environment 3
- Need Max: Hygiene up to 80 (Gussy Up)

### Modart Noudeco Mirror (1-panel)
- Price: $660
- Skill: Charisma (Practice Romance or Practice Speech)
- Need Effects: Hygiene 2 (Gussy Up), Environment 3
- Need Max: Hygiene up to 80 (Gussy Up)

### Modart Noudeco Mirror (3-panel)
- Price: $660
- Skill: Charisma (Practice Romance or Practice Speech)
- Need Effects: Hygiene 2 (Gussy Up), Environment 3
- Need Max: Hygiene up to 80 (Gussy Up)

## Rugs

Rugs are a new category of decorative objects. They're placed, not surprisingly, on the floor and can be walked upon and have objects placed on them.

### Chazz Gassed Incandescent Floor Tile
♦ Price: $30

These special dance floor tiles have several features not present in other rugs. Floor tiles can be configured like the ClubCube (see below) and settings apply to all floor tiles lot-wide. Floor tile settings will not affect ClubCubes on the lot. Configuration has three parts:

- Random Timing: Normally, lights change in a fixed order but this can be altered to change randomly. This control turns random timing on and off.
- Block Fading: When turned on, lights will fade on and off rather than changing cleanly.
- Set Mode: Ten different settings each represent distinct color combinations for floor tiles.

### "Thirsty" the bath mat
♦ Price: $50

### The Fun Spot Kids Rug
♦ Price: $135

### Recherché Floor Runner
♦ Price: $325

### "Unbridled Braids" Oval Rug
♦ Price: $350

### Recalling Rug
♦ Price: $500

### Sung-Gyu Sunburst Oriental Rug
♦ Price: $800

### The Inlaid Medallion
♦ Price: $875

### Recalling Rug 3x3
◆ Price: §1,000

## Miscellaneous

### ClubCube by Luminescent Projections
◆ Price: §65
◆ Need Effects: Environment 5

The ClubCube is a programmable decorative object that can be personalized with different color combinations and light patterns. For full details, see "Chazz Gassed Incandescent Floor Tile," above.

### Juice on the Wall Sculpture
◆ Price: §240
◆ Need Effects: Fun 3 (View), Environment 2
◆ Need Max: Fun up to 95 (View)

### The HottCorp Burning 8-R Series Fire Jet
◆ Price: §325
◆ Need Effects: Environment 2, Fun (Roast Marshmallows)

### note
Fire jets will start fires and burn Sims nearby, so locate them away from flammable objects and, if possible, physically isolate them with fences or other obstacles.

### Interactions:
◆ Turn On/Turn Off: Switches fire jets on or off. If you stagger a bunch of fire jets, they'll continue to fire in the order in which you turned them on.
◆ Roast Marshmallow: Satisfies Fun. Cooking skill dictates whether Sim's marshmallow ignites.

## Plumbing

### Sinks

### Shinytyme Kitchen Sink by Gurglomics
◆ Price: §300
◆ Type: Countertop
◆ Skill: Cleaning (Clean), Mechanical (Repair)
◆ Need Effects: Hygiene 5 (Wash), Hygiene 6 (Sponge Bath), Hunger 1 (Drink)
◆ Need Max: Hygiene up to 90 (Wash), Hygiene up to 25 (Sponge Bath), Hygiene up to 70 (Bathe Baby)

## Electronics

### TVs and Computers

### SwingarmCo 27" Multivid V Television
◆ Price: §750
◆ Skill: Cooking (Watch Yummy Channel), Body (Work Out), Mechanical (Repair)
◆ Need Effects: Fun 7 (varies by Sim's reaction to the channel); Energy -3, Comfort -3, Hygiene -7, (Work Out); Environment 3
◆ Need Max: Depends on Sim's reaction to channel

This wall-mounted TV contains all standard TV features.

## Audio

### Dancing Fiend Jukebox

- ◆ Price: $1,100
- ◆ Skill: Body (Work Out)
- ◆ Need Effects: Fun 9 (Dance Together); Fun 5 (Dance Solo); Fun 3 (Listen to Music—in Bed); Energy -3, Comfort 3, Hygiene -7, (Work Out); Environment 2

◆ Need Max: Fun up to 55 (Dance Solo) or 65 (Dance Together) or 60 (Listen to Music).

### Standard stereo features.

All stereos now feature a new interaction: Dance Smustle. The smustle is a wildly popular group dance that Sims can begin on any audio device or on any Sim already doing the smustle. Every Sim that joins the smustle synchronizes with all other Sims doing the smustle. How well they dance and how many mistakes they make is tied directly to the Sim's hidden dancing skills.

### VocoPhonicSim Karaoke Machine

- ◆ Price: $1,800
- ◆ Skill: Creativity (Sing Solo or Sing With...)
- ◆ Need Effects: Fun 8, Environment 1, Social (Duet)

### Interactions:

◆ Sing: Sim takes to the microphone to belt out a tune. The song is chosen at random and the singing quality is tied to your Sim's Creativity skill. On a home lot it builds Creativity. Children can only perform solo.

◆ Sing With...: Choose a Sim to sing with and he or she will either accept or reject based on Mood, Daily, and Lifetime Relationship, Outgoing/Shy, and Nice/Grouchy (see Chapter 7 for full details). Both Sims get Fun and, if on a home lot, build Creativity. Quality

of singing is tied to each Sim's Creativity skill. On dates, singing a duet is a Date Event that appeals especially to Playful and Romance Sims and less so to Serious and Knowledge Sims.

◆ Dance: Click on the machine when a Sim is singing and Sim dances to the music. Gives Fun and, if other Sims Dance Together, Social.

◆ Watch: Gives Fun and, if more than one Sim is watching, Social. Sims may boo or cheer based on Daily Relationship and singer's Creativity.

### The GrooveLayer 9000 Professional DJ Booth by HotBeats

- ◆ Price: $2,750
- ◆ Skill: Creativity (Be the DJ)
- ◆ Need Effects: Fun 10, Environment 3
- ◆ Need Max: Energy -50 (Be the DJ)

### Interactions:

◆ Dance Solo: Sim dances solo as with any audio object.

◆ Dance Smustle: Sim begins dancing smustle wherever they are on the lot. Other Sims can click on your smustling Sim and join the smustle. Likewise, you can click on other Sims to join with your Sim.

◆ Work as the DJ: Take over for the DJ on a Community Lot; your Sim works the booth and DJ wanders the lot as fully sociable NPC. Performance is tied to your Sim's Creativity skill. While manning the booth, your Sim earns simoleans.

◆ Be the DJ: At home, your Sim can work the DJ booth. He or she won't earn money but he or she will build Creativity skill.

◆ Change Style: While your Sim is working the booth, the style of music can be altered to fast, medium, slow, or House Mix. House Mix pulls MP3s out of your computer's Music folder.

◆ Request...: Changes the style of music to fast, medium, slow, or House Mix.

## Lighting

### Table Lamps

**Romantic Romance by Elle and Eey**
◆ Price: $100
◆ Need Effects: Environment 1

**"Squintimacy" Votive table lamp by Dimview and Co.**
◆ Price: $110
◆ Need Effects: Environment 1

**Mr. Lampy McFourlegs**
◆ Price: $150
◆ Need Effects: Environment 1

### Wall Lamps

**note**

In *The Sims 2 Nightlife*, the Neon Flamingo has been moved from the Decorative/Wall Hangings menu to the Wall Lamps menu.

**"Belle Epoque" Tiffany wall lamp by Frufru Lighting Design**
◆ Price: $50
◆ Need Effects: Environment 1

**Lunatech Light Disc**
◆ Price: $95
◆ Need Effects: Environment 1

**One Pin, Two Pin**
◆ Price: $125
◆ Need Effects: Environment 1

**"Five Diamonds" Wall Light**
◆ Price: $130
◆ Need Effects: Environment 1

**EverGlow Uranium Rod**
◆ Price: $170
◆ Need Effects: Environment 1

Connects with other EverGlow Uranium and Plutonium Rods.

**EverGlow Plutonium Rod**
◆ Price: $175
◆ Need Effects: Environment 1

Connects with other EverGlow Plutonium and Uranium Rods.

**BeamOLite Compacto Wall Lamp by Ray Diant**
◆ Price: $210
◆ Need Effects: Environment 1

### BeamOLite Extendo Wall Lamp by Ray Diant
◆ Price: $225
◆ Need Effects: Environment 1

### "Diamonds Forever" Wall Light
◆ Price: $500
◆ Need Effects: Environment 2

## Hanging Lamps

### The Shadow Streamer
◆ Price: $375
◆ Need Effects: Environment 2

The Shadow Streamer and the Gobo-a-Go-Go Spotlighter (below) are programmable club lights that come in a variety of colors. They can be programmed and manipulated in several ways. First, you can designate which and how many of the lights patterns it will do with the Toggle Animation interaction. Experiment setting several of these lights for different patterns to create just the scene you want for your club. Second, you can stagger when individual lights in a group activate so that they don't flash in unison.

### note
Whenever you load a lot, all these lights are switched on simultaneously and, therefore, flashing in unison. If you're staging a movie or just want to create a particular mood, turn off the lights and switch them on in turn to create a staggered effect.

### The Gobo-a-Go-Go Spotlighter by LumiO
◆ Price: $425
◆ Need Effects: Environment 2

See "The Shadow Streamer," above.

### The Prismo RotoBall by LumiO
◆ Price: $550
◆ Need Effects: Environment 3

## Hobbies
### Exercise

### ElectroDance Sphere by LimIntense Unlimited
◆ Price: $3,500
◆ Skill: Body (Spin), Mechanical (Repair)
◆ Need Effects: Fun 10 (Spin), Fun 8 (Watch), Social (Watch), Social (Be Watched)

Interactions:

◆ Spin: Sim takes the sphere for a spin at your choice of difficulty: easy, medium, and hard. Builds Body skill on home lots. The higher the difficulty, the faster the sphere will spin. The chance of getting ejected from the machine is a function of Body skill versus the level selected (a Body 1 will likely get ejected on medium and high and even on low, while a Body 10 will only occasionally get ejected on high and almost never on medium or low). After spinning, there's a random chance the Sim will throw up; the chance is higher if he or she is ejected. Performance in the sphere is a Date Event that impacts the date in proportion to the speed. Date score is reduced if the Sim is thrown from

the machine (the higher the speed, the greater the loss) and also for throwing up.

◆ Watch: Sims will watch another Sim in the dance sphere and get Fun and Social (if other Sims are watching too). The spinning Sim also gets Social if others are watching and changes in Daily Relationship with any Sims who boo or cheer. Whether a spectator will cheer depends on whether he or she likes the spinning Sim as well as his or her personality. Primarily, however, booing and cheering depends on a comparison of the spinning Sim's Body skill and the speed of the sphere. A Sim spinning at a speed above his or her Body skill is more likely to be cheered, while a Sim spinning at below his or her Body skill is more likely* to be booed. Being booed or cheered is a Date Event, so spectators can add another dimension to the date scoring potential of using the dance sphere.

### note

Strange things can happen in the dance sphere; it doesn't seem to be entirely of this world. There is a very slim chance that Sims who've previously been abducted by aliens will unexpectedly disappear while using the dance sphere. After two hours, they rematerialize just as mysteriously. The more times a Sim has been abducted, the more likely he or she will be to undergo this curiosity.

## Recreation

### "52 Pickup" Card Table

◆ Price: $630
◆ Need Effects: Fun 9 (Play), Fun 4 (Watch), Social (Play and Watch)

**Interactions:**

◆ Play: Sitting at the table, even alone, requires a $100 buy-in. If the Sim sits alone, he or she will play with the cards and the chips for Fun and get his or her $100 back when he or she disengages. If another Sim joins, the game begins. Sims ante $10 and bet $10 per betting round, gaining Social and Fun as

they play. Players can fold before a game is complete. At the end of a game, a Sim collects his or her winnings and a new game begins. Players stay at the table even if their Fun is maxed out. When a player leaves the table, his or her chips are converted into simoleans and added to his or her family funds.

◆ Watch: Sims watch the Sims playing at the table and cheer or boo based on Daily Relationships with the players. Booing decreases Daily Relationship and cheering increases it.

### "Pinmaster 300" Bowling Alley by Hurling Fun Products, Inc.

◆ Price: $5,500
◆ Skill: Body
◆ Need Effects: Fun 10, Social

**Interactions:**

◆ Play: Builds Body skill on home lots. A Sim playing alone will practice, receiving Fun and autonomously exiting when fun is full. If, however, another Sim joins, the practice round becomes an actual game with Sims taking turns for a full 10-frame game. Sims exit when the game is complete. How well a Sim bowls is dictated by his or her Body skill. Up to four Sims can play together with everyone receiving both Fun and Social.

◆ Join: Sims can join a game that doesn't already have four Sims. If only one Sim is playing, a game begins. If more than one Sim is already playing, the new Sim joins the game in progress.

## Miscellaneous

### Party

All island bars are functionally identical to the Way Fluid Island Bar in that they spawn an NPC Bartender when placed on a Community Lot and they connect with matching island counters. When on a home lot, they function just like normal juice bars (e.g., Bachman Busbar).

**note**

The previously Community Lot-only Way Fluid Island Bar from the *The Sims 2 University* expansion pack is now available for home lots under the Miscellaneous Party catalog.

## "The Grease Stands Alone" Island Bar

◆ Price: $1,780

◆ Need Effects: Fun 3

◆ Need Max: Fun up to 50 (Juggle) or 80 (Make Drinks) or 50 (Consume Drinks) or 70–90 (Drink from Bottle, depends on Playful/Serious)

**note**

If you place identical bars side by side, they'll connect.

### Interactions:

◆ Order Drink: Community Lot only. Order a Blended ($15) or Poured ($10) drink from NPC Bartender. Drinking satisfies Fun.

◆ Tend Bar: Community Lot only. Young adult or older can replace the NPC Bartender at the machine and serve any Sims who order drinks. Earn simoleans for time spent working job, awarded when you cancel interaction.

◆ Drink from Bottle: Home lot only. Satisfies Hunger and Fun. Playful Sims get a higher maximum Fun than Serious.

◆ Make a Drink: Home lot only. Satisfies Fun. Prepares single drink.

◆ Make Drinks: Home lot only. Prepares multiple drinks.

◆ Juggle Tumblers: Home lot only. Satisfies Fun.

◆ Join: Home lot only. Join Juggling. Satisfies Fun.

## The Oasis

◆ Price: $1,850

◆ Need Effects: Fun 3

◆ Need Max: Fun up to 50 (Juggle) or 80 (Make Drinks) or 50 (Consume Drinks) or 70–90 (Drink from Bottle, depends on Playful/Serious)

See "The Grease Stands Alone" Island Bar, above.

## "NeonBar" by Neontrix

◆ Price: $2,100

◆ Need Effects: Fun 3

◆ Need Max: Fun up to 50 (Juggle) or 80 (Make Drinks) or 50 (Consume Drinks) or 70–90 (Drink from Bottle, depends on Playful/Serious)

See "The Grease Stands Alone" Island Bar, above.

## Cars

Cars are a new category of objects that set your Sims free of the tyranny of carpools, school buses, and taxis.

Cars require a place to park. At the very least, there must be one main driveway piece for a single car. If the household has multiple cars, there must be at least a main piece per car or a main piece for one car and an extender piece for each additional car. If cars are blocking each other in the driveway, they magically teleport around to the street.

One of the great strategic advantages of a car is that Sims can leave for work or school whenever they please. Not only can they wait to leave until minutes before their shift begins, as they always could with the carpool, but they can even go in late. There is no penalty for being up to

one hour late. Beyond that, however, and the tardiness counts as an absence for job performance and grading purposes though the Sim still gets his or her day's pay. Three tardies and your Sim will be demoted at work.

A Sim with a car can travel to a Community Lot by clicking on the car rather than the telephone (as he or she would to get a taxi). Using a car to travel to Community Lots is faster as there's no time wasted waiting for the cab to come. You may also navigate to a neighboring Community Lot by clicking on it directly (if the Clickable Neighbors option is turned on). If your household has a car but no one in particular owns it, your selected Sim summons a cab. If, however, the car is owned by the active Sim when you clicked on the neighboring lot, he or she will automatically use the car.

All Sims cars have infinite capacity; any number of Sims can fit inside.

Sims can automatically drive as soon as they become teens and can even be the designated owner of a car.

**Interactions:**

◆ **Change Owner:** By default, a car is not owned by any one Sim. Making a Sim (teen or older) the owner, however, has several effects. When a car is assigned an owner, the carpool and/or school bus for that Sim will no longer come. Instead, the Sim automatically routes to the car as work time approaches. Naming an owner does not prevent other Sims using the car for any reason but they'll never use it autonomously. If another Sim has the car when the owner needs to go to work, the carpool shows up as normal so the owner can make it to work on time (as if the household didn't have a car at all). If the owner of the car is left at or restored to "Nobody," no Sim will use the car autonomously and must be directed to do so.

◆ **Drive to Community Lot:** A car can be used in lieu of a taxi to drive to Community Lots. Sims climb in and select Community Lots from their base neighborhood, downtowns, and universities.

◆ **Take a Spin:** A quick one-hour joyride satisfies Fun.

◆ **Drive to Work:** Appears within one hour of a job's start time and remains available until end of the Sim's shift. The interaction appears for all Sims regardless of who owns the car.

◆ **Take to School:** Drive a child or teen Sim to school. The driver returns shortly thereafter. Students return home on the bus.

◆ **Drive to School:** A teen can drive himself to school.

◆ **Carpool to Work With...:** If two or more Sims start work at the same time, you can choose to have all Sims drive to work together in the car. This will not happen autonomously; the Sim to whom the car does not belong will autonomously route to the carpool car instead. To get your Sims to travel together, cancel the carpool for the non-owners, then select Carpool to Work With... for each of the non-owner Sims. If Sims' jobs end at a different time than the car's owner, they'll return home in the normal carpool vehicle.

◆ **Carpool to School With...:** If there's more than one teen or a teen and one or more children in the household, any teen can drive all students to school. However, because high school and elementary school end at different times, the children will return home on the bus while the teens will return in the car.

◆ **Get Alarm Installed:** Car alarm prevents the car being stolen by the Burglar. Sim departs the lot for one hour to have the alarm installed and returns $250 lighter. Thereafter, all Sims will turn off the alarm before getting in.

◆ **Sit in Vehicle:** Sim takes a seat in parked car. Required for availability of in-car interactions, below.

◆ **Turn Stereo On:** Must be sitting in vehicle. Turns on the car stereo.

◆ **Dance:** If the car's stereo is on, any nearby Sim can click on the vehicle and dance. The Sim in the car must first get out before he or she can boogie.

◆ **Turn Lights On:** Must be sitting in vehicle. Turns car lights on.

◆ **Kiss:** Two Sims only must be sitting in vehicle. Standard Kiss interaction.

◆ **Make Out:** Two Sims only must be sitting in vehicle. Standard Kiss interaction.

◆ **WooHoo:** Two Sims only must be sitting in vehicle. Standard

WooHoo interaction. If done while the car is on a Community Lot, this counts as a public WooHoo.

◆ Try for Baby: Two Sims only must be sitting in vehicle. Standard Try for Baby interaction.

◆ Ask to Get Out: Specify a Sim to remove from the car.

### note

Parking the car in a garage and putting a household alarm on the garage has a similar, but less comprehensive, effect as installing an alarm in the car itself. Because a room alarm and a car alarm both cost $250, it'll save multi-car families some money to build a multi-car garage and put one alarm on it instead of on individual cars. However, room-based burglar alarms provide only partial protection against theft, while the car alarm renders a vehicle 100 percent unstealable.

### The Smoogo Minima

◆ Price: $950

◆ Need Effects: Comfort 1 (Sit In) and Fun 2 (Take a Spin)

### The Smord P328

◆ Price: $2,250

◆ Need Effects: Comfort 1 (Sit In) and Fun 4 (Take a Spin)

### The Landwhale by Heaveola

◆ Price: $4,250

◆ Need Effects: Comfort 4, Energy 1 (Sit In) and Fun 2 (Take a Spin)

### The Yomoshoto Evasion

◆ Price: $6,250

◆ Need Effects: Comfort 6, Energy 2 (Sit In), and Fun 5 (Take a Spin)

### Hunka 711 by Hwang Motors

◆ Price: $11,950

◆ Need Effects: Comfort 8, Energy 3 (Sit In), and Fun 9 (Take a Spin)

## Miscellaneous

### "Sit 'n' Grin" Photo Booth from iBurn Commercial Imagery

◆ Price: $1,300

◆ Need Effects: Fun 9

### note

During a date, having a picture taken together on a date is a (for most Sims) positive Date Event. For Shy Sims, however, it's actually a negative Date Event.

#### Interactions:

◆ Get In: Sim gets in photo booth.

◆ Join: If one Sim is in the booth, another playable Sim can click on the booth to share it. Alternately, the playable Sim can click on any other Sim to join him or her in the booth. The other Sim will accept based on Daily and Lifetime Relationship (at least 0 and -100, respectively); acceptance or rejection will impact the Sims' relationship.

◆ Take Picture: For $10 your Sims can take a picture in one of three poses: normal, goofy, and romantic (if there are two Sims inside with at least a crush or love relationship). The Sims gain

Fun. If two Sims get their picture taken, both gain more Fun per Sim. If a Sim is shy, he or she gets no Fun from taking a picture. The picture emerges from the booth and the Sim deposits it in his or her inventory. The picture can be placed on a table or wall on your Sims lot. If there's a single Sim in the booth, and he or she is a vampire, the normal pictures will be special vampire poses.

◆ WooHoo/Try for Baby: Two romantically involved young adult or older Sims in a photo booth with sufficient relationship can attempt these intimate social interactions (just as in a clothing booth). These count as public WooHoos for those Sims who crave such public displays. If Mrs. Crumplebottom is in the room, she'll wait for your Sims to emerge and deliver an epic tirade.

# Community Lot-Only Objects

Many of the objects cataloged above are also available for designing your Community Lots. Some, however, are exclusive to these non-residential destinations.

## Surfaces

**Chiclettina "Fjord" All purpose Counter**
◆ Price: $750
◆ Need Effects: Environment 2

## Decorative

**Signs of Elliptical Joy by Alexandra Workman**
◆ Price: $100
◆ Need Effects: Environment 1

**The Parallelosign by Signalellocrop**
◆ Price: $100
◆ Need Effects: Environment 1

**Restaruant Sign by Upturned Nose**
◆ Price: $100
◆ Need Effects: Environment 10

## Electronics
### Neukum Systems Wall Speakers

◆ Price: $400
◆ Need Effects: Fun 2

These commercial grade speakers produce one kind of music and don't have to be connected to a stereo. They are color-coded to the precise musical genre:

◆ Checkerboard: Neukum Systems "Hep Cat" 50s Rock Wall Speaker
◆ Wood Grain: Neukum Systems "Isorhythm" Classical Wall Speaker

## Miscellaneous

**Tempest Cooktop from Cuas**
◆ Price: $2,500
◆ Need Effects: Hunger 10

Chapter 6

# NEW OBJECTS

This stove is designed for restaurant use only. This stove spawns the NPC Cook who prepares meals in community Lot restaurants; without this object, a restaurant will not function.

### "Gastronomique" Restaurant Podium
◆ Price: $200

This podium is designed for restaurant use only. It spawns both the NPC Host and Server who seat and serve food (respectively) in Community Lot restaurants; without this object, a restaurant will not function.

Interactions:

◆ Be Seated: Begins the restaurant experience by having Host take your Sim to a table.

◆ Skip Out on Bill: Sims can get a free meal if they can stay away from the Host for 45 seconds. If successful, this gives Fun. Only available before meal is done.

◆ Pay Bill/Use Coupon: When meal is done, end the dining experience by paying for the dinner or (if your Sim has one in his or her inventory) using a coupon.

◆ Give Up Seat: If your Sims haven't ordered, they can end the dining experience with no cost by giving up their seats.

### "Compulsion" Fragrance Display
◆ Price: $3,500
◆ Need Effects: Fun 4, Environment 9

This countertop rack sells the potentially Turn On/Turn Off-inspiring Compulsion unisex cologne in quantities of 1, 3, 5, and 10 bottles at §125 per bottle.

Once purchased, the cologne bottles go into your Sim's inventory. They can be held there or placed on the ground for others to pick up and put in their inventory.

To apply Compulsion, click on your Sim and select Use Cologne. The scent adheres to your Sim for 180 minutes but can be removed sooner by a shower, bath, or sponge bath or swimming in a pool.

**note**

The effect of the cologne is represented by the flowers floating around your Sim wherever he or she goes.

Why would your Sim want to wear cologne? Some Sims find cologne to be a Turn On and will be more attracted to Sims wearing it. If you want your Sim to be more attractive to such a Sim, apply some cologne watch your Sim become even more appealing. Note, however, that a Sim could also have cologne as his or her Turn Off, significantly reducing the attractiveness of any Sim who he or she thinks stinks.

Cologne should, therefore, be used strategically only in response to a Sim with a known cologne Turn On.

**tip**

Discover a Sim's Turn Ons and Turn Offs with the Ask...What Turns You On/Off socials.

Because the effect of cologne is temporary, your goal should be to use the fleeting boosted attractiveness to build up the relationship with the Sim you want your Sim to woo. Once the relationship is strong, Attraction no longer matters strategically, so wearing more cologne won't help matters.

## Aspiration Reward Objects

Aspiration reward objects are detailed in Chapter 3.

primagames.com  **85**

# Chapter 7

# New Socials

Prowling around town at night is all about socializing. Dating, outings, bowling, playing cards, eating at restaurants: they're all about interacting with more Sims more often and more intensely. That's why *The Sims 2 Nightlife* introduces several

## Social Interaction Directory

| Interaction | Menu | Availability Daily A to B Above | Availability Daily A to B Below | And/Or | Availability Lifetime A to B Above | Availability Lifetime A to B Below | Crush | Love or Go Steady | Autonomous Personality | User Direct |
|---|---|---|---|---|---|---|---|---|---|---|
| About Grilled Cheese | Talk | -100 | 100 | And | -100 | 100 | — | — | — | Yes |
| About Interests | Ask | -10 | 100 | And | 0 | 100 | Not allowed | Not allowed | — | Yes |
| Apologize | Appreciate | -100 | 100 | And | -100 | 100 | — | — | — | Yes |
| Back to My Place? | Ask | 55 | 100 | And | 30 | 100 | Not allowed | Not allowed | — | Yes |
| Bad Mouth | Talk | 0 | 100 | And | 0 | 100 | — | — | — | Yes |
| Bite Neck | Vampire | 40 | 100 | And | 30 | 100 | — | — | — | Yes |
| Blow Kiss | Dining | 25 | 100 | And | 15 | 100 | Sets | Sets | — | Yes |
| Caress Hands | Dining | 55 | 100 | And | 30 | 100 | Sets | Sets | Nice | Yes |
| Cuddle | Booth | 35 | 100 | And | 25 | 100 | Sets | Sets | — | Yes |
| Dance Close | Slow Dance | 20 | 100 | And | 20 | 100 | — | — | — | Yes |
| Dare to Peek | Coffin | -100 | 100 | And | -100 | 100 | — | — | Outgoing | Yes |
| Do You Like What You See? | Ask | -100 | 100 | And | -100 | 100 | Not allowed | Not allowed | — | Yes |
| Feed a Bite | Dining | 35 | 100 | Or | 25 | 100 | Sets | Sets | — | Yes |
| Hand | Kiss | 30 | 100 | And | 15 | 100 | Sets | Sets | Playful | Yes |
| Head On Shoulders | Slow Dance | 30 | 100 | And | 20 | 100 | Sets | Sets | — | Yes |
| Hot Smooch | Booth | 60 | 100 | And | 45 | 100 | Required | Sets | — | Yes |
| How Much Money Do You Have? | Ask | 25 | 100 | And | 15 | 100 | Not allowed | Not allowed | — | Yes |
| Kiss | Car | 45 | 100 | And | 15 | 100 | Required | Sets | Outgoing | Yes |
| Love Talk | Booth | 40 | 100 | And | 25 | 100 | Sets | Sets | — | Yes |
| Lower Hands | Slow Dance | 45 | 100 | And | 35 | 100 | Sets | Sets | — | Yes |
| Make Out | Car | 80 | 100 | And | 50 | 100 | Required | Sets | Outgoing | Yes |
| On Date | Ask | 0 | 100 | And | 0 | 100 | Not allowed | Not allowed | — | Yes |
| On Outing | Ask | 0 | 100 | And | 0 | 100 | Not allowed | Not allowed | — | Yes |
| Ride Home | Ask | -100 | 100 | Or | -100 | 100 | — | — | — | Yes |
| Slow Dance | Slow Dance | 30 | 100 | And | 15 | 100 | — | — | — | Yes |
| Smooch | Slow Dance | 65 | 100 | And | 45 | 100 | Required | Sets | — | Yes |

dozen new social interactions to weave into your Sims' nightlife.

This chapter lists all new social interactions. The Social Interaction Directory below contains all social availability, autonomy, and social, and relationship impacts; the catalog that follows it goes into detail about which Sims can do the interactions, how the interactions work, and how Sims decide to accept these interactions.

| Autonomous | If Accept, A's Social | If Accept, A's Daily | If Accept, A's Lifetime | If Accept, B's Social | If Accept, B's Daily | If Accept, B's Lifetime | If Reject, A's Social | If Reject, A's Daily | If Reject, A's Lifetime | If Reject, B's Social | If Reject, B's Daily | If Reject, B's Lifetime |
|---|---|---|---|---|---|---|---|---|---|---|---|---|
| Yes | 10 | 5 | 1 | 22 | 4 | 2 | 0 | -10 | -1 | 0 | -7 | -2 |
| Yes | 6 | 1 | 0 | 6 | 1 | 0 | -3 | -2 | 0 | -3 | -2 | 0 |
| Yes | 10 | 5 | 1 | 22 | 4 | 2 | 0 | -10 | -1 | 0 | -7 | -2 |
| Yes | 30 | 14 | 2 | 24 | 10 | 1 | -10 | -8 | -1 | -15 | -10 | -2 |
| ? | 24 | 5 | 0 | 24 | 5 | 0 | 10 | -3 | 0 | 10 | -6 | 0 |
| Yes | 14 | 6 | 2 | 20 | 13 | 2 | -4 | -4 | -2 | -4 | -4 | -2 |
| Yes | 14 | 8 | 1 | 14 | 8 | 1 | 8 | -6 | -1 | 0 | -6 | -1 |
| ? | 20 | 9 | 1 | 20 | 10 | 1 | -4 | -9 | -2 | -3 | -8 | -2 |
| Yes | 20 | 6 | 2 | 20 | 10 | 2 | 0 | -10 | -3 | 0 | -10 | -2 |
| Yes | 20 | 6 | 0 | 18 | 8 | 0 | -5 | -4 | 0 | -2 | -1 | 0 |
| Yes | 22 | 9 | 1 | 6 | 4 | 0 | -10 | -10 | -3 | 0 | -7 | -2 |
| Yes | 0 | 0 | 0 | 0 | 0 | 0 | 0 | 0 | 0 | 0 | 0 | 0 |
| Yes | 20 | 10 | 1 | 16 | 9 | 1 | -6 | -8 | -1 | 0 | -6 | -1 |
| Yes | 16 | 9 | 1 | 16 | 9 | 1 | 8 | -6 | -1 | 0 | -6 | -1 |
| Yes | 16 | 5 | 1 | 16 | 6 | 1 | 0 | -5 | -1 | 0 | -7 | -1 |
| Yes | 22 | 13 | 2 | 20 | 11 | 2 | 0 | -11 | -2 | 0 | -12 | -3 |
| ? | 30 | 13 | 1 | 30 | 6 | 1 | -10 | -7 | -1 | -15 | -10 | -1 |
| No | 18 | 10 | 2 | 16 | 10 | 2 | 8 | -8 | -2 | 0 | -10 | -2 |
| Yes | 18 | 6 | 1 | 18 | 8 | 1 | 0 | -7 | -1 | 0 | -8 | -1 |
| Yes | 18 | 10 | 2 | 16 | 10 | 2 | 8 | -8 | -2 | 0 | -8 | -3 |
| Yes | 30 | 19 | 5 | 30 | 19 | 5 | 8 | -15 | -4 | 0 | -15 | -4 |
| No | 14 | 6 | 0 | 20 | 4 | 0 | 0 | -5 | 0 | 0 | -5 | 0 |
| No | 10 | 1 | 1 | 22 | 4 | 2 | 0 | -10 | -1 | 0 | -7 | -2 |
| Yes | 18 | 8 | 0 | 18 | 8 | 0 | -5 | -4 | 0 | -5 | -3 | 0 |
| Yes | 22 | 13 | 2 | 20 | 11 | 2 | 0 | -11 | -2 | 0 | -12 | -3 |

## Social Interaction Directory continued

| Interaction | Menu | Availability Daily A to B Above | Availability Daily A to B Below | And/Or | Availability Lifetime A to B Above | Availability Lifetime A to B Below | Crush | Love or Go Steady | Autonomous Personality | User Directed |
|---|---|---|---|---|---|---|---|---|---|---|
| Steal a Bite | Dining | -100 | 100 | Or | -100 | 100 | — | — | — | Yes |
| Surprise Engagement | Dining | 75 | 100 | And | 70 | 100 | Required | Required | — | Yes |
| Throw Drink | Irritate | 15 | 15 | And | 10 | 10 | — | — | — | Yes |
| Throw Drink | Dining | 15 | 15 | And | 10 | 10 | — | — | — | Yes |
| Throw Food | Dining | -100 | 100 | And | -100 | 100 | — | — | Playful? | Yes |
| Toast | Dining | 20 | 100 | And | 10 | 100 | — | — | — | Yes |
| What Are Your Skills? | Ask | -20 | 100 | And | -10 | 100 | Not allowed | Not allowed | — | Yes |
| What Do You Want/Fear? | Ask | 15 | 100 | And | 5 | 100 | Not allowed | Not allowed | — | Yes |
| What Is Your Job? | Ask | 7 | 100 | And | 0 | 100 | Not allowed | Not allowed | — | Yes |
| What Turns You On/Off? | Ask | 5 | 100 | And | 0 | 100 | Not allowed | Not allowed | — | Yes |
| What's Your Sign? | Ask | -100 | 100 | And | -100 | 100 | Not allowed | Not allowed | — | Yes |
| WooHoo | Car | 85 | 100 | And | 65 | 100 | Required | Required | Outgoing | Yes |
| WooHoo | Photo Booth | 85 | 100 | And | 65 | 100 | Required | Required | Outgoing | Yes |

# Sim-to-Sim Interactions

## Ask Interactions

### About Interests

◆ Who: Teen/young adult/adult/elder to teen/young adult/adult/elder

Ask About Interests

**note**

Sim flashes the icons of his or her top three interests. If the Sim has a Grilled Cheese Aspiration, he or she will display his or her only interest: grilled cheese, of course.

Always accepted.

## Do You Want a Ride Home?

◆ Who: Young adult/adult/elder to young adult/adult/elder or teen to teen

**note**

Community Lot only. Works the same as End Date but automatically returns your Sim and date to their respective homes.

Always accepted.

## Do You Want to Go Back to My Place?

◆ Who: Young adult/adult/elder to young adult/adult/elder

# New Socials

| Autonomous | If Accept, A's Social | If Accept, A's Daily | If Accept, A's Lifetime | If Accept, B's Social | If Accept, B's Daily | If Accept, B's Lifetime | If Reject, A's Social | If Reject, A's Daily | If Reject, A's Lifetime | If Reject, B's Social | If Reject, B's Daily | If Reject, B's Lifetime |
|---|---|---|---|---|---|---|---|---|---|---|---|---|
| Yes | 8 | 5 | 0 | 6 | 3 | 0 | 8 | -3 | 0 | 0 | -4 | 0 |
| No | 100 | 6 | 3 | 100 | 9 | 3 | -30 | -15 | -5 | -4 | -8 | -4 |
| Yes | 8 | -7 | -3 | -10 | -13 | -4 | — | — | — | — | — | — |
| Yes | 8 | -7 | -3 | -10 | -13 | -4 | — | — | — | — | — | — |
| Yes | 10 | 8 | 1 | 8 | 8 | 1 | 8 | -6 | -1 | 0 | -6 | -1 |
| Yes | 14 | 6 | 0 | 14 | 10 | 0 | — | — | — | — | — | — |
| ? | 10 | 1 | 0 | 10 | 1 | 0 | -4 | -1 | 0 | -4 | -1 | 0 |
| ? | 14 | 9 | 0 | 20 | 13 | 0 | -4 | -4 | 0 | -4 | -4 | 0 |
| ? | 10 | 5 | 0 | 10 | 5 | 0 | -4 | -3 | 0 | -4 | -3 | 0 |
| ? | 14 | 4 | 0 | 14 | 4 | 0 | -4 | -2 | 0 | -4 | -4 | 0 |
| Yes | 10 | 1 | 0 | 10 | 1 | 0 | -4 | -1 | 0 | -4 | -1 | 0 |
| No | 50 | 13 | 8 | 50 | 13 | 8 | 0 | -12 | -5 | 0 | -15 | -5 |
| No | 50 | 13 | 8 | 50 | 13 | 8 | 0 | -12 | -5 | 0 | -15 | -5 |

**note**
Community Lot only. This social is the only way to return to your Sim's lot from a Community Lot while on a date without prematurely ending the date.

Accepted if Sim A is Attraction-eligible for Sim B and Sim B's:

**1.** Mood >-20, Daily >70, and Lifetime >40, or

**2.** Mood >40, Daily >70, Lifetime 36–40, Outgoing/Shy >7, or

**3.** Mood >40, Daily >70, Lifetime 36–40, Nice/Grouchy >7, or

**4.** Mood >-20, Daily 61–70, Outgoing/Shy >7, and Lifetime >30.

## Do You Like What You See

◆ Who: Young adult/adult/elder to young adult/adult/elder or teen to teen

**note**
This social reveals whether and why they're attracted to your Sim. See Chapter 4 for details.

Always accepted.

## How Much Money Do You Have?

◆ Who: Teen/young adult/adult/elder to teen/young adult/adult/elder

**note**
The questioned Sim reveals his or her wealth level with one of three "§" symbols: § for low wealth, §§ for medium wealth, and §§§ for high wealth.

# The Sims 2 Nightlife Expansion Pack

Accepted if Sim A is Attraction-eligible for Sim B and Sim B's:

1. Mood >-20, Lifetime <25, Nice/Grouchy <7, and Daily >50, or

2. Mood >-20, Lifetime 21–25, Nice/Grouchy >7, Daily 30, or

3. Mood >-20, Lifetime >25, Daily >45, or

4. Mood >40, Lifetime >25, Daily 31–45, Nice/Grouchy >7, or

5. Mood >40, Lifetime >25, Daily 31–45, Nice/Grouchy <7, Outgoing/Shy >6.

## On Date

- Who: Young adult/adult/elder to young adult/adult/elder or teen to teen

**note**

See Chapter 5 for details.

Accepted if Sim A is Attraction-eligible for Sim B and Sim B's:

1. Attracted, Mood >-20, Daily >15, Lifetime >7, or

2. Attracted, Mood >40, Daily >15, Lifetime 1–6, and Outgoing/Shy >7, or

3. Attracted, Mood >40, Daily >15, Lifetime 1–6, Outgoing/Shy <7, and Nice/Grouchy >7, or

4. Attracted, Mood >-20, Daily 8–15, Outgoing/Shy >7, and Lifetime >5.

## To Form/Join Casual Group

- Who: Young adult/adult/elder to young adult/adult/elder or teen to teen

**note**

See Chapter 5 for details.

Accepted if Sim B's:

1. Daily >5 and Mood >10, or

2. Daily <5 and Lifetime >0.

## What Are Your Skills?

- Who: Young adult/adult/elder to young adult/adult/elder or teen to teen

**note**

The Sim will reveal his or her highest-ranking skill in the following terms:

- "I'm pretty good at...": skill 1–3

- "I'm very good at...": skill 4–7

- "I'm an expert at...": skill 8–10

If the asked Sim has no skills, he or she will say "I'm not really good at anything yet."

Accepted if Sim B's:

1. Mood >-20, Daily >5, and Daily >0, or

2. Mood >30, Daily >5, Lifetime -4–0, and Outgoing/Shy >7, or

3. Mood >30, Daily >5, Lifetime -4–0, Outgoing/Shy <7, or Neat/Sloppy >7, or

4. Mood >-20, Daily <5, Outgoing/Shy >7, Daily >-5, Lifetime >-2.

## What Do You Fear?

◆ Who: Young adult/adult/elder to young adult/adult/elder or teen to teen

 **note**
Asked Sim reveals one randomly selected Fear, displayed as an icon and as text.

Accepted if Sim B's:

1. Mood >-20, Daily >20, Lifetime >8, or

2. Mood >20, Daily >20, Lifetime 1–8, Outgoing/Shy >7, and Sim A is Attraction-eligible, or

3. Mood >20, Daily >20, Lifetime 1–8, Outgoing/Shy <7, Nice/Grouchy >7, and Sim A is Attraction-eligible, or

4. Mood >-20, Daily <20, Outgoing/Shy >7, Daily >5, and Lifetime >0.

## What Do You Want?

◆ Who: Young adult/adult/elder to young adult/adult/elder or teen to teen

 **note**
Asked Sim reveals one randomly selected Want, displayed as an icon and as text.

Accepted if Sim B's:

1. Mood >-20, Daily >20, Lifetime >8, or

2. Mood >20, Daily >20, Lifetime 1–8, Outgoing/Shy >7, and Sim A is Attraction-eligible, or

3. Mood >20, Daily >20, Lifetime 1–8, Outgoing/Shy <7, Nice/Grouchy >7, and Sim A is Attraction-eligible, or

4. Mood >-20, Daily <20, Outgoing/Shy >7, Daily >5, and Lifetime >0.

## What Turns You Off?

◆ Who: Young adult/adult/elder to young adult/adult/elder or teen to teen

 **note**
Asked Sim reveals the icon of their Turn Off.

Accepted if Sim A is Attraction-eligible for Sim B and Sim B's:

1. Mood >-20, Daily >30, and Lifetime >20, or

2. Mood >40, Daily >30, Lifetime 16–20, Outgoing/Shy >7, or

3. Mood >40, Daily >30, Lifetime 16–20, Outgoing/Shy <7, and Nice/Grouchy >7, or

4. Mood >-20, Daily 26–30, Outgoing/Shy >7, or Lifetime >12.

# The Sims 2 Nightlife — Expansion Pack

## What Turns You On?

◆ Who: Young adult/adult/elder to young adult/adult/elder or teen to teen

**note**

Asked Sim reveals the icon of one randomly selected Turn On.

Accepted if Sim A is Attraction-eligible for Sim B and Sim B's:

1. Mood >-20, Daily >30, and Lifetime >20, or
2. Mood >40, Daily >30, Lifetime 16–20, Outgoing/Shy >7, or
3. Mood >40, Daily >30, Lifetime 16–20, Outgoing/Shy <7, and Nice/Grouchy >7, or
4. Mood >-20, Daily 26–30, Outgoing/Shy >7, or Lifetime >12.

## What's Your Job?

◆ Who: Young adult/adult/elder to young adult/adult/elder or teen to teen

**note**

Asked Sim reveals the icon for his or her career and his or her specific job title.

Accepted if Sim B's:

1. Mood >-20, Daily >13, and Daily >5.

2. Mood >30, Daily >13, Lifetime -4–5, and Outgoing/Shy >5, or
3. Mood >30, Daily >13, Lifetime -4–5, Outgoing/Shy <5, or Nice/Grouchy >5, and
4. Mood >-20, Daily 11–13, Outgoing/Shy >7, and Lifetime >0.

## What's Your Sign?

◆ Who: Young adult/adult/elder to young adult/adult/elder or teen to teen

**note**

Sim reveals his or her zodiac sign. Zodiac sign provides a rough estimate of the other Sim's personality traits. See Chapter 4 for details on translating zodiac sign into personality traits.

Accepted if Sim A is Attraction-eligible for Sim B and Sim B's:

1. Mood >-20, Outgoing/Shy >6, and Daily >10, or
2. Mood >-20, Outgoing/Shy <6, and Daily >-20, or
3. Mood >0, Outgoing/Shy <6, Daily <-20, and Nice/Grouchy >6.

## Buy Off

◆ Who: Young adult/adult/elder to young adult/adult/elder or teen to teen

**note**
When a romantic rival (see Chapter 9) is trying to muscle in on your Sim's date or loved one, this interaction will dispatch the intruder for the remainder of the current date. Sims can be bought off for §50.

Always accepted.

## Bite Neck

◆ Who: Young adult/adult/elder vampire to teen/young adult/adult/elder or teen to teen

**note**
Used to convert other Sims into vampires.

Accepted if Sim A is Attraction-eligible for Sim B and Sim B's:

1. Daily >20 and Knowledge Aspiration, or
2. Not Knowledge Aspiration and Daily >95, or
3. Not Knowledge Aspiration, Daily 81–95, and Logic >9, or
4. Not Knowledge Aspiration, Daily 61–80, and Logic >6, or
5. Not Knowledge Aspiration, Daily 41–60, and Logic >3.

## Kiss Interactions

### Kiss Hand

◆ Who: Young adult/adult/elder to young adult/ adult/elder or teen to teen

Accepted if Sim A is Attraction-eligible for Sim B and Sim B's:

1. Mood >-40, Daily >35, and Lifetime >20, or
2. Mood >25, Daily >35, Lifetime 4–20, and Playful/Serious >7, or
3. Mood >25, Daily >35, Lifetime 4–20, Playful/Serious <7, and Nice/Grouchy >7, or
4. Mood >-40, Daily <35, Playful/Serious >7, Daily >5, and Lifetime >5.

## Irritate Interactions

### Bleh!!!

◆ Who: Teen/young adult/adult/elder vampire to teen/young adult/adult/elder

**note**
Sims react with the same fear response as with ghosts. Other vampires will Bleh!!! back.

Always accepted.

## Throw Drink

◆ Who: Teen/young adult/adult/elder to teen/young adult/adult/elder

 **note**
Can't be rejected but reaction depends on receiving Sim's personality. Can be done seated or standing.

Always accepted.

## Flirt Interactions

### Check Sim Out

◆ Who: Young adult/adult/elder to young adult/adult/elder or teen to teen

 **note**
Reveals amount of your Sim's Attraction to a specified Sim. Like all Flirt interactions, Check Sim Out affects your Sim's gender preference. See Chapter 4 for details.

Always accepted.

## Talk Interactions

### Bad Mouth

◆ Who: Young adult/adult/elder to young adult/adult/elder or teen to teen

 **note**
If Sim A is Furious at Sim B (see Chapter 9), Sim A can bad mouth B to a third Sim, Sim C. C will either accept or reject the interaction based on Sim C's Nice/Grouchy (the nicer the Sim is, the less likely he or she is to accept Bad Mouth) and his or her relationships to both B and A. The friendlier the Sim is with A, the more likely he or she is to accept and the friendlier he or she is with B, the more likely the Sim is to reject. If accepted, this interaction increases C's Daily Relationship with A and damages it toward B. If rejected, C's relationship with A decreases.

Accepted if Sim B's:

1. Daily >15, Nice >7, and Lifetime >10, or

2. Daily >15, Nice >7, Lifetime <10, and Mood >-10.

## Slow Dance Interactions

The slow dance can be done anywhere to any music or no music at all. It's just a romantic thing to do.

Once two Sims are slow dancing, several other interactions (detailed) can further affect the relationship and/or Date Score. These nested interactions can only be done during a slow dance.

Depending on the receiving Sim's personality and how many rejected Slow Dance interactions occur, the other Sim may decide to end the dance. How he or she does so depends on personality:

◆ Mean: Slap     ◆ Serious: Yell At

◆ Nice: Cry      ◆ Playful: Poke

All Slow Dance socials are romantic interactions that will inspire jealousy if another loved Sim is present.

## Slow Dance

◆ Who: Young adult/adult/elder to young adult/adult/elder or teen to teen

 **note**
Available anywhere even if there's no music source on the lot.

Accepted if Sim A is Attraction-eligible for Sim B and Sim B's:

1. Mood >60, Daily >35, and Lifetime >20.

2. Mood >30, Daily >35, Lifetime 11–20, Outgoing/Shy >7, or

3. Mood >30, Daily >35, Lifetime 11–20, Outgoing/Shy <7, and Nice/Grouchy >7, or

4. Mood >60, Daily 26–35, Outgoing/Shy >7, Lifetime >20.

## Dance Close

◆ Who: Young adult/adult/elder to young adult/adult/elder or teen to teen

 **note**
Only available during slow dance.

Accepted if Sim A is Attraction-eligible for Sim B and Sim B's:

1. Mood >-30, Daily >35, and Lifetime >25.

2. Mood >40, Daily >35, Lifetime 11–25, Outgoing/Shy >7, or

3. Mood >40, Daily >35, Lifetime 11–25, Outgoing/Shy <7, and Nice/Grouchy >7, or

4. Mood >-30, Daily 31–35, Outgoing/Shy >7, Lifetime >20.

## Lower Hands

◆ Who: Young adult/adult/elder to young adult/adult/elder or teen to teen

 **note**
Only available during slow dance.

Accepted if Sim A is Attraction-eligible for Sim B and Sim B's:

1. Mood >-20, Daily >55, and Lifetime >35.

2. Mood >40, Daily >55, Lifetime 21–35, Outgoing/Shy >8, or

3. Mood >40, Daily >55, Lifetime 21–35, Outgoing/Shy <8, and Playful/Serious >9, or

4. Mood >-20, Daily 36–55, Outgoing/Shy >9, Lifetime >35.

## Head on Shoulder

◆ Who: Young adult/adult/elder to young adult/adult/elder or teen to teen

**note**
Only available during slow dance.

Accepted if Sim A is Attraction-eligible for Sim B and Sim B's:

1. Mood >-20, Daily >40, and Lifetime >25.

2. Mood >30, Daily >40, Lifetime 16–25, Outgoing/Shy >7, or

3. Mood >30, Daily >40, Lifetime 16–25, Outgoing/Shy <7, and Nice/Grouchy >7, or

4. Mood >-20, Daily 31–40, Outgoing/Shy >7, Lifetime >25.

## Smooch

◆ Who: Young adult/adult/elder to young adult/adult/elder or teen to teen

**note**
Only available during slow dance.

Accepted if Sim A is Attraction-eligible for Sim B and Sim B's:

1. Mood >-20, Daily >70, and Lifetime >45.

2. Mood >30, Daily >70, Lifetime 25–45, Outgoing/Shy >8, or

3. Mood >30, Daily >70, Lifetime 5–45, Outgoing/Shy <8, and Playful/Serious >9, or

4. Mood >-20, Daily 56–70, Outgoing/Shy >8, Lifetime >35.

# Self Interactions

## Scope Room

The Sim scans his or her current room to find the Sim he or she finds the most attractive. Note that this social does not read *Chemistry* but rather *Attraction* of your Sim to another. For more info, see Chapter 4.

This interaction should be always available. If it's not, your Sim has not yet done anything to set gender preference. To set it, do the unrejectable Flirt interaction Check Sim Out to any Sim of the gender you'd like your Sim to prefer. Thereafter, Scope Room will appear on the Interaction menu when you click on your own Sim.

## Primp

This self-inter-action increases Hygiene and can be done when standing or seated. For most Sims, Primp is user-directed only. For Outgoing and Neat Sims and for the Diva and Mr. Big NPCs, it is also an autonomous interaction and a reflection of their concern with their appearance.

If a vampire Primps, he or she will hiss at the mirror (which, of course, doesn't show his or her reflection) and get a reduction in Comfort instead of an increase in Hygiene. Beware, therefore, if your vampire Sim is both Outgoing and Neat because, unlike other Sims, he or she will Primp autonomously, driving down his or her Comfort.

# Object-Based Interactions

## Espresso Bars

### Buy Espresso For

Click on any espresso bar to invite for coffee any Sim on the lot that your Sim knows.

Accepted if Sim B's:

1. Mood >-35, Outgoing/Shy >6, and Daily >-10, or
2. Mood >-35, Outgoing/Shy <6, and Daily >10.

## Dining Tables/Counters

While Sims sit at dining tables or counter islands either at home or on Community Lots, they may now do several new Dining social interactions. These special interactions are marked in the interactions menu with a gold chair-shaped icon.

For most of these interactions, Sims must be seated either next to or across from each other,

not diagonally. They must also be sitting at the table, not scooted back from the table (as a Sim does when there's a dirty or serving plate blocking his or her place).

### Kiss...Blow Kiss

◆ Who: Young adult/adult/elder to young adult/adult/elder or teen to teen

Accepted if Sim A is Attraction-eligible for Sim B and Sim B's:

1. Mood >-40, Daily >30, and Lifetime >20.
2. Mood >20, Daily >30, Lifetime 6—20, Outgoing/Shy >7, or
3. Mood >20, Daily >30, Lifetime 6—20, Outgoing/Shy <7, and Nice/Grouchy >7, or
4. Mood >-40, Daily 6—30, Outgoing/Shy >7, Lifetime >20.

### Flirt...Caress Hands

◆ Who: Young adult/adult/elder to young adult/adult/elder or teen to teen

Accepted if Sim A is Attraction-eligible for Sim B and Sim B's:

1. Mood >-40, Daily >50, and Lifetime >35.

**2.** Mood >30, Daily >50, Lifetime 6–35, Outgoing/Shy >7, or

**3.** Mood >30, Daily >50, Lifetime 6–35, Outgoing/Shy <7, and Nice/Grouchy >7, or

**4.** Mood >-40, Daily 26–50, Outgoing/Shy >7, Lifetime >25.

## Flirt...Feed a Bite

◆ Who: Young adult/adult/elder to young adult/adult/elder or teen to teen

### note
There must be food on the table.

Accepted if Sim A is Attraction-eligible for Sim B and Sim B's:

**1.** Mood >-40, Daily >40, and Lifetime >30, or

**2.** Mood >20, Daily >40, Lifetime 6–30, Outgoing/Shy >7, or

**3.** Mood >20, Daily >40, Lifetime 6–30, Outgoing/Shy <7, and Nice/Grouchy >7, or

**4.** Mood >-40, Daily 6–40, Outgoing/Shy >7, Lifetime >20.

## Play...Steal a Bite

◆ Who: Teen/young adult/adult/elder to teen/young adult/adult/elder

### note
There must be food on the table.

Accepted if Sim A is Attraction-eligible for Sim B and Sim B's:

**1.** Mood >-10 and Daily >55, or

**2.** Mood >-10, Daily 36–55, Neat/Sloppy >6, or

**3.** Mood >-10, Daily 1–35, Neat/Sloppy >4.

## Propose...Surprise Engagement

◆ Who: Young adult/adult/elder to young adult/adult/elder

### note
This interaction can be a major dream-date maker or breaker.

Accepted if Sim B's:

**1.** Lifetime >75, Daily >75, and Mood >0, or

**2.** Lifetime 71–75, Nice/Grouchy >9, and Mood >0, or

**3.** Lifetime >75, Daily <75, Nice/Grouchy >7, and Mood >0.

## Play...Throw Food

◆ Who: Teen/young adult/adult/elder to teen/young adult/adult/elder

**note**

If the receiving Sim is Playful, he or she will fight back. There must be food on table.

**Accepted if Sim B's:**

. Mood >-10 and Daily >55, or

. Mood >-10, Daily 36–55, and Neat >6, or

. Mood >-10, Daily 1–35, and Neat >4.

## Irritate...Throw Drink

See Throw Drink under Irritate Interactions, above.

## Entertain...Toast

◆ Who: Teen/young adult/adult/elder to teen/young adult/adult/elder

**note**

In the Toast social, Sim A is the Sim proposing the toast. Sim B is any other Sim at the table, and Sim C is the Sim whose honor the toast is being made.

If a Sim B rejects the toast, he or she will boo the toastee.

**Accepted if:**

. Sim B's Daily to Sim C >20, Sim B's Daily to Sim A >20, Sim B's Mood >0, or

. Sim B's Daily to Sim C >20, Sim B's Daily to Sim A >20, Sim B's Mood <0, and Sim B's Nice/Grouchy >5, or

. Sim B's Daily to Sim C >20, Sim B's Daily to Sim A >-20, Sim B's Mood >20, or

4. Sim B's Daily to Sim C >20, Sim B's Daily to Sim A -9–20, Sim B's Mood <20, Sim B's Nice/Grouchy >7, or

5. Sim B's Daily to Sim C >-10, Sim B's Daily to Sim A >40, Sim B's Daily to Sim C >30, and Sim B's Mood >60, or

6. Sim B's Daily to Sim C >-10, Sim B's Daily to Sim A >40, Sim B's Daily to Sim C >30, Sim B's Mood <60, and Sim B's Nice/Grouchy >8, or

7. Sim B's Daily to Sim C >-10, Sim B's Daily to Sim A >40, Sim B's Daily to Sim C <30, and Sim B's Mood >60, or

8. Sim B's Daily to Sim C >-10, Sim B's Daily to Sim A >40, Sim B's Daily to Sim C >30, Sim B's Mood <60, and Sim B's Nice/Grouchy >8.

## Booths

Dining booths (specifically the Jacuster's "Last Stand" Sectional Booth) contain many of the same interactions as sofas plus a few new ones. Functionally, they work just like sofa- and bed-based interactions; once both Sims are sitting in the booth, all available nested interactions (marked by a target-shaped icon) show in the Interaction menu.

For all booth interactions, Sims must be seated adjacent and can't be in the middle of dining at a restaurant.

### Cuddle

◆ Who: Young adult/adult/elder to young adult/adult/elder or teen to teen

Accepted if Sim A is Attraction-eligible for Sim B and Sim B's:

1. Daily >45, or

2. Daily <45, Nice/Grouchy >7, Lifetime >35, and Mood >50.

## Hot Smooch

◆ Who: Young adult/adult/elder to young adult/adult/elder or teen to teen

Accepted if Sim A is Attraction-eligible for Sim B and Sim B's:

1. Mood >-20, Daily >70, and Lifetime >45, or

2. Mood >30, Daily >70, Lifetime 25–45, Outgoing/Shy >8, or

3. Mood >30, Daily >70, Lifetime 5–45, Outgoing/Shy <8, and Playful/Serious >9, or

4. Mood >-20, Daily 56–70, Outgoing/Shy >8, Lifetime >35.

## Love Talk

◆ Who: Young adult/adult/elder to young adult/adult/elder or teen to teen

Accepted if Sim A is Attraction-eligible for Sim B and Sim B's:

1. Mood >-30, Daily >50, and Lifetime >35.

2. Mood >30, Daily >50, Lifetime 20–35, Outgoing/Shy >8, or

3. Mood >30, Daily >50, Lifetime 20–35, Outgoing/Shy <8, and Playful/Serious >9, or

4. Mood >-30, Daily 36–50, Outgoing/Shy >8, Lifetime >25.

# Karaoke Machine

The new Karaoke machine object enables your Sims to invite another Sim to join your Sim in a song.

## Sing Duet

◆ Who: Teen/young adult/adult/elder to teen/young adult/adult/elder

### note

Singing duets can contribute to Date Score.

Accepted if Sim B's:

1. Mood >-20, Daily >25, and Lifetime >15.

2. Mood >30, Daily >25, Lifetime 6–15, Outgoing/Shy >7, or

3. Mood >30, Daily >25, Lifetime 6–15, Outgoing/Shy <7, and Nice/Grouchy >7, or

4. Mood >-20, Daily 16–25, Outgoing/Shy >7, Lifetime >10.

## Vampire Coffin

### Dare to Peek

◆ Who: Teen/young
adult/adult/elder
to teen/young
adult/adult/elder

**note**

Depending on the degree of the scare,
this can cause peekers to wet their
pants, flee, or die of fright.

### Accepted if Sim B's:

1. Mood >-20, Nice/Grouchy >7, Lifetime >20, and Daily > 30, or

2. Mood >70, Nice/Grouchy >7, Lifetime 1–20, and
Daily >70, or

3. Mood >-20, Nice/Grouchy <7, Lifetime >50, and Daily
>40, or

4. Mood >70, Nice/Grouchy <7, Lifetime <50, Lifetime >20, and
Daily >70.

## Photo Booth

### Join in Photo
Booth

◆ Who: Child/
teen/young
adult/adult/elder to
child/teen/young
adult/adult/elder

### Accepted if Sim B's:

1. Mood >-20, Nice/Grouchy >7, Lifetime >20, and Daily > 30, or

2. Mood >70, Nice/Grouchy >7, Lifetime 1–20, and Daily >70, or

3. Mood >-20, Nice/Grouchy <7, Lifetime >50, and Daily >40, or

4. Mood >70, Nice/Grouchy <7, Lifetime <50, Lifetime >20, and
Daily >70.

## Cars

Car interactions contain
nested interactions
including:

◆ Kiss
◆ Make Out
◆ WooHoo
◆ Try for Baby

# Chapter 8

# New NPCs

Whenever Sims venture outside the comfort of their cozy neighborhoods, they can always count on meeting some interesting new people. Not surprisingly, *The Sims 2 Nightlife* is full of extremely interesting new folks.

This chapter guides you through these new characters, outlining what they can (and can't) do, and how you can use them to make your Sims' lives more interesting, challenging, or successful.

# Social NPCs

## Service NPCs
### Gypsy Matchmaker

- ◆ Call Hours: 24 hours
- ◆ Shift: N/A
- ◆ Fee: Variable
- ◆ Service: One Time

The Gypsy Matchmaker is a purveyor of potions and a magical arranger of romance. She's always a female elder and can be found by chance in many public places and even summoned like any other service NPC. Unlike most service NPCs, however, she's on call 24 hours a day.

This mystical Sim appears on Community Lots in base, downtown, and college neighborhoods or can be summoned by cell or home phone (using the Services menu) to any base or downtown neighborhood.

### note
The Gypsy Matchmaker also drops by your Sims' homes the first time you play the lot after installing this expansion pack. She informs you about the handy ReNuYu Porta-Chug potion that's been placed in each preexisting Sim's inventory. This potion gives every Sim a free chance to alter his or her randomly assigned Turn Ons and Turn Offs.

Use any phone to summon the match-maker to work her amorous mojo.

The Gypsy Matchmaker's primary function is to turn two strangers into a match made in heaven. Use the Ask for Blind Date interaction (specifying which gender you'd like the date to be) to retain her matchmaking services. The price for this service is not fixed, but rather a donation. The truth, however, is that the more you pay, the better the match will be.

- ◆ $0–$250: Bad match
- ◆ $250–$500: Good match
- ◆ $500: Great match

### note
Once the matchmaker arrives, any Sim on the lot can engage her services. In fact, the Sim that called her need not take any notice of her at all. Someone will, however, have to greet her or she'll wander off.

How much you pay determines the level of Chemistry your Sim and the blind date will share.

When the matchmaker makes a match, she considers every non-engaged/non-steady townie (base neighborhood) and downtownie of your Sim's preferred gender with whom your Sim has a relationship, ranking them by their Chemistry with your Sim. The more you pay, the higher ranked Sim you'll get as a match. Full price, for example, always gets you a high-Chemistry Sim. Below §250, you get a Sim with no attraction to your Sim at all.

**note**

Recall that Chemistry is the average of the Attraction between your Sim and another Sim. If your Sim is highly attracted to a Sim but she's cool in return, Chemistry will be somewhere in the middle.

This pool includes the Diva/Mr. Big, the Slob, most service NPCs (e.g., Maid, Mail Carrier), and (occasionally) the Grand Vampire.

...om. Ouch. Hey, wanna go smustle?

When the deal is done, your dream date literally falls from the sky and the date begins.

The matchmaker is your source for two very important potions.

Even if a blind date is not your Sim's desire, the Gypsy Matchmaker also sells two very useful and powerful potions. These potions go into your Sim's inventory for use as needed. They can be removed by placing them on a lot or by drinking them:

◆ Love Potion #8.5: When consumed, this temporarily increases other Sims' Attraction to your Sim. If drunk while another Love Potion is still active, it causes several bad reactions including setting other Sims' Attraction to your Sim to minimum. See Chapter 4 for full details.

◆ Vamprocillin-D: When consumed by a vampire, this potion returns the Sim to normal. If drunk by a non-vampire, it has no effect.

The Gypsy Matchmaker can be interacted with like all other service NPCs. This means she is potentially marriable/joinable. Once a Gypsy Matchmaker becomes part of a household, however, she no longer sells potions or matchmaking services.

## Autonomous NPCs

**note**

Because they're such busy Sims, Servers, Hosts, and DJs are not included when your Sim Scopes the Room for attractive Sims—even if they are, in fact, the most attractive Sims on the lot. To find out if a Server, Host, or DJ shares good Chemistry with your Sim, use the Flirt...Check Sim Out interaction when the Sim isn't engaged in his duties. To evaluate Hosts, however, you have to meet them away from work (because they're *always* engaged in their duties); asking them for a seat adds them to your Sim's Relationship panel, allowing them to be called, invited, and Checked Out later.

### Server

The Server is part of the restaurant dining experience. Once your Sims are seated in a restaurant, the Server arrives to take your Sim's order.

While they wait for your Sims to order, Servers make small talk, building relationships while your Sims make up their minds.

You can socialize with the Server while he or she's on duty, particularly when waiting to take your Sims' order. In fact, one of the most efficient times for Server socializing is before you actually

place an order. The Server waits by your Sim's table indefinitely, autonomously chatting until you actually order food.

**note**

You can't do any interactions with the waiting Server, but your Sims will be building a relationship as they and the server chat automatically.

The direct benefit of making nice with the Servers is that it reduces the chance of their accidentally spilling food on your Sim.

Relationship with a Server is damaged by anything that normally decreases Relationship scores but also when you try to leave a restaurant lot without paying your bill (even by accident) or actually getting caught trying to skip out on the bi

### Host

The Host and his podium are where the restaurant experience begins. To begin dining, click on either the podium or the Host himself and ask to be seated.

To end your Sim's meal, click on the Host or the podium and elect to pay the bill, use a coupor or attempt to skip out on the bill. Skipping out is available only *before* your Sim(s) finish eating; once they're done, the interaction disappears.

Hosts can be powerful friends because they can, on their own initiative, comp all or part of your bill on any given visit. The better your Sim's relationship with a Host, the more likely he'll be t comp the bill and the larger a proportion of the bill he'll comp.

Relationship with the Host is damaged in all the usual ways but also by attempting to leave the lot without paying the bill (even by accident) and by getting caught trying to skip out on the bill.

## DJ

The DJ appears wherever there's a DJ booth on a Community Lot.

> **note**
>
> DJ booths on home lots don't come with a DJ nor can you hire one to work your Sims' parties.

Like Baristas and Bartenders, the DJ works tirelessly unless your Sim elects to take on DJ duties. When one of your Sims mans the booth, the DJ wanders the lot, available for socializing.

## Non-Social NPCs

### Restaurant Cook

Wherever there's a restaurant stove, there's a restaurant Cook. The restaurant Cook has one function: fill orders in the restaurant. He can't be distracted from this duty nor drawn into any interaction whatsoever. There is one way to add a Cook to your Relationship panel and fully interact with him, but it's a matter of chance: get him as your Sim's blind date from the matchmaker.

## Downtownies

### Mrs. Crumplebottom

Mrs. Crumplebottom is, as she'd freely admit, a busybody and a prude. You may be surprised to know, however, that she has interests beyond verbal tirades and purse beatings.

The curmudgeonly elder Sim shows up frequently but at random on any Community Lot in any kind of neighborhood. Generally, she wanders the lot behaving like any other townie—until, that is, she spies a public display of affection.

The very sight of open canoodling sets her blood aboil and compels her to make an example of the offending exhibitionists. If any romantic interaction is performed in the same room when she isn't otherwise engaged (more on that later), she'll hustle right over, deliver a very stern lecture, and (unless it's physically impossible) repeatedly wallop your Sim with her purse. This withering handbag assault drives down your Sim's Comfort and severely impacts any current outing or date score.

**note**

If your Sim's date is Nice or has a Family Aspiration, the damage from getting Crumplebottom-ed is lessened but still pretty serious. If the date is Mean or has a Popularity or Romance Aspiration, the harm will be even worse.

Crumplebottom doesn't just hate PDAs, she also blows a gasket when Sims are inappropriately dressed. If your Sim is hanging around a Community Lot in undies or swimwear (even if there's a pool), they'll be prime targets for Mrs. Crumplebottom.

Clearly, her presence makes having a successful date a bit more challenging. If you spot her on the lot, be careful to hold your romantic interactions until she's out of the room. Alas, the time limitations of dates don't always allow for this kind of discretion; you have to take your opportunities when they arise.

**note**

Recall that a room is defined in the game as any space delineated by walls and accessed through either a door or an arch. Anything beyond any entryways is a different room. When outside, the entire outdoor area is a single room, though distance can make a difference. Beyond a certain distance, a Sim is too far away to react even if she is in the same room.

The good news is there are a few things she loves more than imposing her moral code on others: bowling, drinking at bars, and playing cards. A lot with any of these features will keep her quite busy and her nose out of your Sim's business. If you spy her in the bowling lanes, at the card table, or bellied up to the bar, smooch away!

As befits her behavior, Mrs. Crumplebottom's personality is Mean, Neat, Shy, and Serious.

Mrs. Crumplebottom offers only limited interactions and isn't marriable/joinable. Attempting to interact with her is, in fact, another opportunity to witness her disdain for other Sims. Try to chat her up and she'll wag her finger at your Sim or whip out her knitting and tune him out completely.

## Grand Vampire

The Grand Vampires (one male and one female) appear at random on Community Lots but only in downtown neighborhoods and only at night. When the sun rises, they emit smoke and flee the lot for the protection of their coffins.

While on the lot, however, they behave largely like any other Sims except for their occasional tendency to turn into bats and greet Sims with a hearty "Bleh!!!"

Grand Vampires offer the full range of interactions and can be befriended and married/joined. If, however, your Sim develops a relationship with a Grand Vampire (Daily Relationship toward your Sim 40 or higher, depending on your Sim's Logic skill), there's a chance the vampire will do the Bite Neck interaction, turning your Sim into a creature of the night.

Find full information on the life of the Sim vampire in Chapter 10.

## Diva/Mr. Big

The Diva and Mr. Big are potentially lucrative but difficult dating challenges. Manage to marry/join them and their fortune and top-level income become part of your household. Getting there, however, may be difficult.

### note

In all respects save gender and appearance, Mr. Big and the Diva are identical.

Also, the names "Diva" or "Mr. Big" refer to them as characters. In the actual game, they're given unique first and last names.

Functionally, these Sims are just like any other townie, but their distinctive appearance is your clue to much more about them. For example, all Divas and Mr. Bigs share the following characteristics:

◆ Aspiration: Fortune
◆ Outgoing/Shy: 10
◆ Nice/Grouchy: 0
◆ Wealth: $$$$
◆ Career: Slacker 10 (Professional Party Guest)
◆ Signature Behavior: Priming, Bragging, Flirting with other Sims
◆ Best Dating Activity: Dancing in a Group, Dates Out

## The Slob

The Slob isn't as big a prize as the Diva/Mr. Big, but is a...um...challenge nonetheless.

All Slobs, regardless of gender, share these characteristics:

◆ Aspiration: Pleasure
◆ Active/Lazy: 0
◆ Neat/Sloppy: 0
◆ Wealth: $
◆ Career: Slacker 2 (Gas Station Attendant)
◆ Signature Behavior: Farting, Spitting, Belching, Sloppy Eating
◆ Best Dating Activity: Dining, Couple Dancing, Dates at Home

## Downtownies in General

The randomly generated townies that inhabit downtown neighborhoods are basically the same as those in base neighborhoods, but they make somewhat better "catches."

They always have level 6 or higher jobs and more money and higher skills than the average base neighborhood townies.

The trick, however, is figuring out which Sims are downtownies and which are plain old townies from your base neighborhood. If you've been playing a neighborhood for a long time, you'll probably recognize most or all your base neighborhood townies, so any unfamiliar faces are likely downtownies.

The most reliable way to pinpoint a downtownie is to use Ask interactions to determine their skills. If none of their skills are very high, they're not a downtownie.

# Chapter 9

# NEW RELATIONSHIPS: FURIOUS, RIVALS, AND CONTACTS

The dynamics that govern how Sims relate to one another are rich and wonderfully complex. Now, however, that tapestry has just gotten a bit richer and more intricate with three new wrinkles: the furious state, rivals, and contacts.

This chapter explains these new relationships and how they fit in both the game and the other new features of the *The Sims 2 Nightlife* expansion pack.

## The Furious State

In days past, Sims didn't hold grudges. Sure, acts of betrayal or physical violence would severely damage relationships, rendering previously routine interactions out of reach until the relationship could be mended. No matter the size of the affront, however, there was no lingering, seething anger for wrongs done.

That fiery thought balloon means this is a furious Sim.

With the new "furious state," however, Sims will remember slights and outright assaults for a fixed time and react accordingly to a Sim who's done them wrong.

When a Sim (let's call him "Sim B") does something offensive to your Sim ("Sim A"), your Sim can become furious at that Sim. This means Sim A's Daily and Lifetime Relationships with the offending Sim B are temporarily—often dramatically—reduced.

The amount of the reduction and the duration of the effect are both proportional to the degree of the wrong. Getting slapped, for example, causes a small and brief reduction, while being caught cheating triggers a massive, long-lasting drop.

**note**

If Sim B does more than one fury-inspiring act, the furious states don't pile up. Instead, if a later furious state has a greater impact than the existing furious state, it replaces the previous one. If, on the other hand, the existing furious state is greater than the new one, the new one is ignored.

The Relationship panel shows at which Sims your Sim is furious. Hint: it's the red one.

When your Sim is furious at another Sim, that Sim's portrait is tinted red in the Relationship panel until the effect subsides. Further, the Daily and Lifetime Relationship score of your Sim toward the offending Sim will be shown in its reduced state.

Over time, the furious state decays and slowly restores the points deducted from the Relationship scores. The effect, however, never reaches zero until the act's duration has passed.

 As a fury ages, the red color recedes counterclockwise.

As the furious state's duration passes, the red tint sweeps away counterclockwise. When there's no red left, the furious state is done.

Both the portrait and the Daily and Lifetime Relationship numbers will return to normal when the furious effect wears off. Note, however, that the relationship numbers may not be exactly what they were before the affront; any interactions your Sim has had with the object of his or her fury during the furious state will change the relationship.

> **note**
>
> If you're not mindful of what furious Sims are doing, they can seriously worsen their relationship with an offending Sim. They'll pick fights, shove, and be generally unpleasant if they're of the correct temperament. Thus, when the effect wears off, the lifting of the furious state may not improve the relationship too much thanks to any damage done under its influence.

## Furious State Aging

The furious state's duration ages any time either Sim A or Sim B is present in the household or Community Lot you're playing. Aging happens while either Sim is present as a playable Sim, a visitor, a walk-by, or as a non-playable townie on a Community Lot.

 Apologizing makes a furious state pass more quickly.

There is one other way to accelerate the aging of a furious state. The furious state is reduced when Sim B performs the Appreciate... Apologize interaction. Though your Sim may do this social as many times as you like, it affects the furious state only once per hour. Other uses after the one per hour have the normal relationship effects but won't impact the furious state.

## Acts That Invoke the Furious State

Several actions cause the furious state, each with a distinct impact (the amount it reduces Daily and Lifetime Relationship) and duration (how long the effect will last).

> **note**
>
> Both a furious act's impact and duration can be altered from the numbers below based on the Furious Sim's Nice/Grouchy personality. A grouchy Sim (Nice/Grouchy 0) sees a larger impact for a longer time (+50%) while a Nice Sim (Nice/Grouchy 10) sees both a shorter impact and a quicker duration (-50%). Sims with Nice/Grouchy 5 will see the effect as detailed below and Sims with scores above and below 5 will see proportionally larger changes the closer they are to the extremes.
>
> Additionally, if the Furious Sim is a child, the duration of his fury will be shorter still than the number listed below, even when accounting for the child's Nice/Grouchy trait.

## Events that Trigger the Furious State, Strength and Duration

| Furious Event | Strength (-Daily and -Lifetime) | Duration (in Hours) |
|---|---|---|
| Be Broken Up with (Marriage) | 175 | 336 |
| Be Broken Up with (Steady) | 100 | 168 |
| Be Burgled (toward Burglar) | 150 | 336 |
| Be Left at Altar | 175 | 336 |
| Being Stood Up | 50 | 48 |
| Conflicting Date Jealousy | 125 | 168 |
| Date couldn't pay for dinner | 50 | 48 |
| Date Jealousy (toward Sim B) | 125 | 168 |
| Date Jealousy (towards Sim C) | 75 | 96 |
| Family Member Cheated (toward cheater A) | 75 | 72 |
| Family Member Cheated (toward cheater C) | 50 | 72 |
| Fight...Attack, lost | 75 | 72 |
| Fined (toward Fireman or Police) | 100 | 72 |
| Get Cheated on (toward cheater A) | 125 | 168 |
| Get Cheated on (toward cheater B) | 75 | 96 |
| Got Drink Thrown in Face | 30 | 12 |
| Got Shoved | 25 | 36 |
| Got Slapped | 50 | 48 |
| Had to clean somebody's puddle andis Neat/Sloppy > 7 | 25 | 12 |
| Lost a game and is Nice/Grouchy < 3 | 25 | 3 |
| Viewing a loved one's Date reward object | 75 | 6 |

 **note**

If Sim A is in a romantic relationship with Sim B and goes on a date with Sim C without B's knowledge, A can still get in trouble for the indiscretion. If A gets a Date reward from C and places it in the household (as opposed to in his inventory) or if B takes delivery of the object, it inspires jealousy just as it would if B stumbled upon the date in progress. Fittingly, this also makes the cuckolded Sim Furious at Sim A.

## Effects of the Furious State

A furious Sim can be pretty darn angry. Several behaviors and effects result from a furious state.

Two Sims, so recently friends, can attack each other mere moments later if one is furious.

◆ Furious Sims frequently show a flaming thought balloon of the Sim at whom they're furious and an icon representing the offense about which they're furious.

◆ Furious sleeping Sims dream of the offender with the same flaming thought balloon.

◆ When a Sim is furious, all interactions normally reserved for enemies (e.g. Attack) become automatically available regardless of relationship levels.

◆ If the offending Sim is a playable Sim, any Sim who is furious at him or her can randomly walk by his or her house and commit an act of vandalism. The furious Sim may kick over the trash can, steal the newspaper, or kick or steal a flamingo or gnome.

◆ If Sim B attempts to interact with Sim A and Sim A rejects, Sim A will show a fiery thought balloon.

◆ If Sim A and Sim B are both in the same room, there's a good chance Sim B will be "driven" from the room by the sheer social awkwardness. These "bad vibes" occur because all advertising scores for every object and interaction in the room inhabited by the furious Sim drop for Sim B (e.g. the TV doesn't advertise as much fun to B as it normally would). Thus, actions outside the room have greater attraction despite being farther away. The effect you see, however, is Sim B staying out of an angry Sim's way.

◆ A furious Sim has a new interaction: Talk...Bad Mouth. This allows the furious Sim to talk smack about Sim B to another Sim. For full detail on Bad Mouth, see Chapter 7.

◆ Furious Sims are very likely to become romantic rivals and try to horn in on an offending Sim's date or loved one.

## Rivalry

All's fair in love and war and that's why Sims can become romantic rivals.

If your Sim is on a date or has a Crush, Steady, Love, or Married relationship with a Sim who's present on the lot, it's possible that some other Sim will try to horn in on your Sim's beloved. How does it happen and what can your Sim do about it?

## How Rivals Are Made

A rival ("Sim C") will set upon your Sim's ("Sim A") love interest ("Sim B") if he or she is attracted to Sim B. How attracted Sim A has to be to behave in this unseemly manner, however, depends on several different qualifications.

**note**
In all the cases listed here (and in any case of rivalry), all three Sims—your Sim, his or her date/paramour, and the rival—must be present on the same lot.

◆ If Sim C is furious at Sim A, he or she will hit on Sim B if he or she is at least neutrally (~10) attracted to Sim B.

◆ If Sim C is not furious at Sim A but is not a friend of Sim A, Sim C will hit on Sim B if he or she is very strongly (150) attracted to Sim B.

◆ If Sim C is a friend of Sim A and isn't furious at Sim A, Sim C will never hit on Sim B.

◆ If Sim C is married/joined/steadied, Sim C may still hit on Sim B but the required Attraction will be greater (increased by 200).

◆ If Sim C is married/joined/steadied *and* a Family Aspiration Sim, Sim C will never hit on Sim B.

◆ If Sim C is a Romance Aspiration Sim, all required Attractions are lowered, meaning it takes *less* Attraction (reduced by 75) for them to become rivals.

**note**
When Sim C becomes a romantic rival, romantic interactions with Sim B advertise to Sim C at an amplified level, making them more attractive interactions than they'd be otherwise.

## Dealing with Rivals

If a rival moves in on your Sim's date/paramour, there are three things your Sim can do:

Greasing a rival's palm gets rid of him for a while.

◆ Influence: If you have enough Influence (1,000 points), using the Influence to...Leave Us Alone social will keep him away for at least six hours. As with all Influence interactions, Daily Relationship must be above -50.

◆ Bribery: Using the Buy Off interaction, you can pay a rival to go away for at least six hours. The amount required to buy him off is $50.

◆ Fisticuffs: To permanently eliminate a romantic rival, your Sim can use the Fight...Attack interaction. This social is always available on romantic rivals but the normal rules apply to who will win (usually the Sim with higher Body skill). If your Sim wins, the rival get a memory of the shameful event and will *never* be a rival to your Sim ever again. If your Sim loses, the other Sim continues to be a romantic rival.

A fight isn't the only answer but, if a rival is being particularly persistent, it may be the best one. Just make sure your Sim has higher Body skill.

**note**
Though the Fight may seem like a good solution, remember that Date score can be damaged even if your Sim wins the Fight. If the date is, for example, very Nice and a Family Sim, the Fight will bring down Date score. If, on the other hand, the date is very Mean and a Popularity Sim, the Fight will substantially help the Date score.

## Contacts

After an outing or a date, your Sim may get a call from a Sim he or she doesn't know, thus creating a temporary relationship called a "contact." Contacts can be extremely useful for the social game but also for other aspects as well.

The calling Sim explains that he or she is a friend of one of the Sims from the previous outing. For the next several hours—depending on how good the date or outing was—this Sim (whom your Sim has yet to actually meet) is added to your Sim's Relationship panel as a contact.

### Date/Outing Score and Resulting Contact Duration

| Date Score | Outing Score | Contact Duration |
|---|---|---|
| OK | So-So | 12 hours |
| Good | Fun | 24 hours |
| Great | Super | 48 hours |
| Dream Date | Rockin' | 52 hours |

**note**
Contacts appear in your Sim's Relationship panel with their portraits shaded blue. When their contact status runs out, they lose their blue hue and become normal acquaintances. The erstwhile contact remains in the Relationship panel at whatever Daily/Lifetime Relationship he or she was when the contact period ended even if your Sim has still never met him or her. There's some decay from the initial relationship numbers, depending on how long the contact period lasted.

If, during the contact period, your Sim becomes furious with a contact, the contact period ends and is replaced by the furious state.

Contacts display in the Relationship panel much like rivals, but they're colored blue instead of red.

Contacts are kind of like temporary friends. From the moment they become a contact, your Sim has an elevated Daily (+30) and Lifetime (+10) Relationship with the contact even if they never subsequently interact. Thus, your Sims can begin relationships with contacts using far more potent interactions than with Sims they barely know. Even more importantly, though contacts aren't actual friends, they count toward the number of friends needed for job promotion and Influence capacity.

# New Relationships: Furious, Rivals, and Contacts

**note**

Because contacts are temporary, they make a useful but shaky foundation for your career and Influence game, though they're more problematic for the latter.

Friends required for jobs matter only at the time of promotion; falling below the required number of friends after the promotion doesn't result in a demotion. If, therefore, a contact expires before your Sim actually befriends him, your Sim won't lose any promotions gained thanks to the contact's contribution to your Sim's friend count. Your Sim won't, however, be eligible for promotion again until he or she replaces the expired contact and meets any additional friend requirements.

Friends required for Influence capacity, however, are more precious. If a contact expires, reducing your Sim's friend count, and your Sim's number of friends is no longer enough for his or her current Influence capacity, that capacity level and any Influence points amassed within it are lost.

The lesson is: don't base your friend count too much on contacts, and befriend contacts before they expire.

The best way to handle contacts is to make them actual friends as quickly as you can. Interact with them extensively and promptly; their significant initial relationship with your Sim should make that easy. When your Sim achieves an actual friend relationship, losing the contact status has no effect save the change in the color of their Relationship panel portrait.

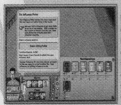

Influence can be elevated if you have a lot of contacts, but it's a temporary boost unless you quickly turn your contacts into friends.

Fortunately, contacts try to make socializing easy. The first time a contact calls, he or she will invite your Sim on a new outing.

If you choose to go on this outing, waiting for you at the destination will be the new acquaintance and the mutual friend mentioned in the phone call, along with either other members of the previous outing's group or a random selection of Sims your Sim knows.

**note**

You may, of course, choose to not send your Sim on the contact's offered outing without impacting the relationship with the contact. You will, however, miss an easy opportunity to socialize with the Sim while he or she is still a contact.

# Chapter 10

# THE LIFE VAMPIRIC

Something fearsome and dark has invaded your Sim's neighborhoods from the shady recesses of downtown. These undead beasts, few in number at first, can spread in time into every quiet street and sleepy cul-de-sac of your Sims' world.

The good news is vampires are a load of fun to be around and, frankly, to become; the cure is just a matter of buying a potion. Sure being a creature of the night requires compromises and some changes in routine, but there's no better nightlife than the undead nightlife.

This chapter explains how to become a vampire, how Sim existence is different for vampires, and how to stop being one.

## Becoming a Vampire

When you first install the *The Sims 2 Nightlife* expansion pack, there are only two vampires in each downtown neighborhood: the male and female Grand Vampires. These shadowy figures appear at random, exclusively on downtown Community Lots and, of course, only at night.

A vampire. In fact, this is one of the original Grand Vampires.

Vampires can be recognized by their pale skin, red eyes, and fangs. The Grand Vampires in particular are iconically dressed in "classic" vampire garb and their names are always preceded by either "Count" or "Contessa."

After a while, any Sim can be vamped, making them look something like this.

## note

Functionally, vampire "skin" is not actually a skin but rather a whole body tattoo. Thus, it cannot be passed on genetically or used as a skin tone for new Sims or in *Body Shop*.

Get too friendly with the local creatures of the night and your Sim will become one too.

If one of your Sims builds a sufficiently high relationship with a Grand Vampire or any of their undead progeny—after at least one of your playable Sims has been bitten, others can also be bitten and become vampires. Once that happens, the whole neighborhood is fair game.

**note**

It is possible to have an (almost) entire neighborhood of vampires but it won't happen automatically. Because townies are not replaced when they are "vamped," the population is not affected by the number of vampires in its midst. To completely vamp a neighborhood, however, your playable Sims will have to do most of the biting because townie vampires (including the Grand Vampires) can convert only 10 percent of the populace. Even with diligent nape-biting, however, you can't make every soul in the neighborhood into a vampire because anytime an NPC (e.g., Gardener or Maid) is vamped, he or she gets replaced by a living Sim. Your vampire utopia will just have to make do with a warm-blooded service sector.

The Grand Vampires will not autonomously bite any Sims until one of your playable Sims has been bitten. After that, they and any townies they vamp will build relationships and bite other townies freely but only until about 10 percent of the Sims in a neighborhood are vampires. Once this ceiling is reached, any further vampire expansion must be done by you and your playable Sims.

**note**

Whether your Sim will get bitten by a vampire depends on several factors including your Sim's Daily Relationship with the vampire (the higher it is, the greater the chance of a successful bite), whether your Sim is a Knowledge Aspiration Sim (Knowledge Sims get bitten at lower Daily Relationships), whether the vampire is the correct age and non-family (required for some but not all conditions), and your Sim's amount of Logic skill (the higher the Logic, the greater the Daily Relationship must be). See Chapter 7 for details.

Once your Sim is bitten, he or she immediately becomes a vampire.

## Vampires at Night

Sim vampires at night can party nonstop; their Needs never decay.

When the sun goes down, there are no more ardent revelers than the vampires. Unlike your average Sim, vampires can party all night without needing to eat, sleep, go to the bathroom, or shower; their Needs don't decay after sunset.

**note**

This doesn't mean that vampires can't be in a bad Mood, just that their Needs don't naturally decline over time. Objects and interactions can still deplete their Needs and, thus, drag down their Mood.

Furthermore, any Need depletion that occurred during the daytime has to be replenished before Needs and Mood can be full. For example, if a vampire needed to use the toilet just before sunset, he or she still needs to after sunset; the Need just won't get any worse. To fulfill the Need and stop its downward pull on his Mood, he or she still must take a potty break.

Thus, until the sun comes up in the morning, vampires have the unusual luxury of doing anything they please without having to stop to tend to their Needs.

Such a state makes socializing easier because (once they top off any Needs depleted before sunset) vampires' Moods are always high. It can also make promotions easier to get because a vampire can work skills without interruption or (if their job starts at night) always leave for work with a top-shelf Mood.

## Vampires in the Daytime

When the sun rises in the morning, vampires become just like any other Sim...if, that is, every other Sim bursts into flames when standing outside—which they don't.

A vampire in the sun begins to sizzle and smoke. Wait too long to get her inside and she'll be history.

If vampires venture outdoors or are caught outside when the sun rises, something very dire happens—their Needs begin to drop very, very quickly. If they remain in the sunshine until their Needs reach rock bottom, they'll suddenly combust and die (again).

### note
A sun-destroyed vampire can still be brought back to life by the Resurrect-O-Nomitron from the <I>The Sims 2 University<I> expansion pack. The resurrected Sim comes back as a vampire or, if you don't spend enough money on the resurrection, as a zombie vampire. Not that we recommend such a cruel fate, but think of the possibilities!

Going to a day job can be very painful for a vampire Sim.

Attached garages, however, really come in handy because your Sim can go from house to car without going outside.

Vampires should, therefore, venture outside only when absolutely necessary. If, for example, the vampire Sim has a job during the day, he or she can still go to work, but the run to the car could be harrowing.

### tip
Make sure a vampire's Needs are filled before running for the carpool during daytime. If his or her Needs are too low when he or she leaves the house, he or she might not make it to the shelter of the car.

Vampires should consider houses with attached garages so they can go directly from the house to the car without braving daylight. Thus can they avoid the Mood-damaging Need decay en route to work and its negative impact on job promotion.

A vampire can function during the day, but he'll have to spend a lot of time tending to his faster-than-normally decaying Needs.

As long as a vampire stays inside, his or her Needs decay faster than normal Sims, but not as precipitously as they would outdoors.

### note
The light from windows does not affect vampire Sims indoors, so there's no need to draw the blinds or paint the windows black.

Also safe is a Sim's car, even if it's parked outdoors. While sitting in the car, the vampire is considered indoors and therefore subject to vampire indoor (faster than normal Sims' but slower than in sunlight) Need decay.

Vampires do have one advantage during the day that can stop their daylight Need decay: the coffin.

## The Vampire Coffin (a.k.a. "The Deep Sleeper")

The coffin allows your vampire to take refuge during the day and freeze their motive decay until sunset.

When vampires sleep in a coffin, their Needs stop decaying just as they do at night. Meanwhile, the vampire's Comfort and Energy replenish just as they would in a normal bed. Of course, they can't do anything productive during this time, but nobody said being a vampire makes life simpler.

If you choose, you can use the coffin to rest your vampire all day, only bringing him out at night when he's at the peak of his abilities. This is thanks to the special way vampires sleep in coffins.

### note
During the day, vampires never accept an invitation or a date via phone.

Normally, an undisturbed Sim sleeps in a bed until his or her Energy Need is full, arising automatically when fully rested. Vampires in coffins, however, stay in their coffin until sunset even if their Energy Need is fulfilled. When the sun goes down, they arise of their own initiative.

### note
You can roust a sleeping vampire early by using the Arise interaction on the coffin.

During the day, most vampires are drawn to sleeping in the coffin. Because doing so prevents your Sim from unwisely wandering outside in the sun, this can be the safest place to be.

### tip
If vampires want to WooHoo at home, they still need a double bed (or a car); coffins are single beds only.

### note
Find full details on the coffin bed in Chapter 6.

# Other Vampire Facts of Life (err...Death)

Several other interesting realities come with being a vampire.

Vampires cast no reflection. Creepy!

Vampires:

◆ Don't reflect in mirrors.

◆ Have their own Irritate social: Bleh!!!

◆ Can turn other Sims into vampires with the Bite Neck social.

◆ Have two special modes of locomotion: Stalk Here and Fly Here. Fly Here transforms your Sim into a bat and is especially useful because (like teleport) it's instantaneous and ignores an intervening obstacles and objects.

◆ Don't age; they (with two exceptions) remain in their current age group forever. If, however a teen vampire goes to college, he or she becomes a young adult vampire. Likewise, a vampire who graduates from college becomes an adult. They will, however, never age again.

◆ Can't starve to death or drown.

◆ Can reproduce. Vampirism is not hereditary and pregnant vampires have normal children.

◆ Produce a special set of photos when they use the photo booth object.

One of the coolest vampire abilities is the Fly Here mode of travel. You may not recognize your Sim in this state, but she'll get where she's going really fast.

# Curing Vampirism

### note

If you want to summon the matchmaker in order to buy a potion, you're still calling her for matchmaking services. Once she arrives, however, she's available for either service and there's no obligation to set up a blind date.

Vampirism can be cured at any time by buying a vial of Vamprocillin-D from the Gypsy Matchmaker. The potion can be bought when your Sims encounter her on a Community Lot or by calling her to your Sim's home.

### tip

Because potions are kept in your Sim's inventory rather than consumed immediately, you can buy a vial of Vamprocillin-D any time and use it if your Sim needs to be cured quickly. You can even buy in bulk (up to 10 bottles).

Once a vampire Sim consumes a vial of Vamprocillin-D, he or she instantly returns to normal. If a non-vampire drinks this potion, it has no effect but does disappear from his or her inventory.

If you want to cure a non-controllable Sim and your Sim has sufficient influence, he or she can influence another Sim to take Vamprocillin-D.

## Chapter 11

# BUILD MODE ADDITIONS

The more varied kinds of lots you'll want for your downtown call for new features in Build mode. This chapter lays out the various new features and refined existing features that you'll see in The Sims 2 Nightlife.

## New Lot Sizes

Several new lot sizes, big and small, expand your possibilities by granting you different canvases on which to create your architectural work of art.

The new lot sizes add new dimensions to your community and residential spaces.

- ◆ 3x1: $900
- ◆ 2x2: $1,600
- ◆ 2x3: $2,900
- ◆ 2x4: $4,200
- ◆ 5x2: $5,500
- ◆ 5x6: $18,500

## 1/2 Walls

1/2 walls are a brilliant way to break up a space without creating a new room.

Use 1/2 walls to partially delineate a space within a larger room.

These new dividers are found within the Wall tool panel and come in a variety of colors and configurations. Some are just unfinished half-height walls with colored trim on the top. Others actually extend higher than waist height, with either panes of glass or wooden spindles comprising their upper half.

**note**
You can hang ceiling lights directly above 1/2 walls.

The bottom portion of the 1/2 wall is unfinished and will accept any wall covering.

Some 1/2 walls have upper portions made of glass or wooden spindles. These segments can be seamlessly combined with standard low 1/2 walls.

No matter which variety of 1/2 wall you employ, each comes in a variety of colors with unfinished wall portions that can be covered like a normal wall. What's more, different styles of 1/2 walls intelligently join at intersections to form even more interesting combinations.

Like fences, 1/2 walls can be joined at almost any angle.

You can't insert either doors or gates into 1/2 walls, so leave or cut spaces for Sims to walk through.

Though you'll find them staggeringly useful, there are several things 1/2 walls can't do:

◆ They don't delineate a "room" for Environment score or any other gameplay purpose. For example, if a Sim commits a jealousy-inspiring act with the potentially jealous Sim on the other side of a 1/2 wall, the jealous Sim is still considered to be in the same room and, therefore, aware of the betrayal. The reason for this should be obvious: a 1/2 wall doesn't entirely block view, so anyone on the opposite side of one can see quite clearly.

◆ For the same reason, 1/2 walls don't block light.

◆ Despite their superficial similarity to fences and traditional walls, 1/2 walls cannot support a door or gate. To create pass-throughs, leave gaps in the 1/2 walls or delete segments of finished 1/2 walls.

◆ Because they don't reach the ceiling, 1/2 walls can't bear weight and therefore, can't provide support for floors above.

# Driveways and Garages

To have a car, a Sim must first have a driveway. The tools for this project are in the new Garage menu in Build mode.

Driveways are built using two different parts: the driveway itself and extenders.

The main driveway piece must be adjacent to the road and far enough away from the lot's right side. This piece is too close.

This one is just right!

The initial driveway piece comes in two surfaces: concrete (in asphalt and gray colors) or brick (red and yellow colors). For placement, it must physically touch the street in front of your Sim's lot. You'll notice when placing this L-shaped piece that it requires a lot of space and specific conditions:

◆ There must be seven tiles between the right side of your lot and the left edge of the driveway to give space for a car to approach from the right and turn onto the lot.

- There must be open space 10 tiles deep from the street.
- There must be clearance five tiles wide for the length of the piece.

If any of these conditions are lacking, you won't be able to place the driveway.

Extender pieces take the driveway farther back on the lot. Notice that the surface of the extender can be different from the main piece.

Once you choose a valid location, you may just stop there; the end piece is all you need to be able to buy a car. If, however, you wish the driveway to extend farther back on the lot, you'll need an extender. Extenders can be made of either material (they aren't required to match the main piece) and lengthen the driveway by eight tiles.

Garage doors must be placed between a main driveway piece and an extender or between two extenders. They can't cut through the middle of a piece or be placed at the end with no driveway beyond them.

The next question that presents itself is whether you want to build a garage. Or, more precisely, whether you want to build a garage door. Garage doors can be placed only on the joint between two driveway/extender pieces. To finish the garage, build walls around the entire extender

piece adjacent to the door. The walls must enclose the entire piece (8 tiles long by 10 tiles wide) because walls can't cut across the middle of the extender pieces.

## note
If you build a garage door (even with no walls enclosing the garage) your Sim will always park the car beyond the door unless an object or another Sim is beyond the door and blocking the path.

Apart from the garage door, the actual garage structure is optional. If you want one, just build walls at least the length of one (or more) extender piece and any width you please.

Walls, like garage doors, can't cut across the middle of a driveway piece.

If your garage is wider than the driveway piece it encloses, lay down matching floor cover on the extra tiles.

## note

You cannot build a garage around a basic driveway piece, only around extender pieces.

**tip**

Make a garage larger than the driveway piece by laying floor tiles around it that match the surface of the driveway ("Asymmetric Tesselations in Umbre" or "Square Off in Ochre" for brick and "Sid's Cement" flooring or "Terrific Tarmac" asphalt for concrete).

For multiple cars, either configuration will work.

To have more than one car in the household, each must have its own driveway piece. Thus, a two-car household must have either a main driveway piece and an extender or two side-by-side main pieces. If two cars share a single-width driveway, they magically work around each other if one is blocking the other.

For multi-car garages, lay main driveway pieces side by side.

Then, place two garage doors and build the garage structure.

Because driveway pieces can be laid next to each other, you can create any number of side-by-side garages or driveways, each with its own garage door.

Instead of a garage, you can build a carport by constructing columns around the driveway and laying roof-ish floor tiles above it. To manage it, however, you need to be a bit tricky:

Build a foundation extending beyond (7 x 7 tiles, one tile back from the curb) the place you plan to put your driveway.

Build a wall where your carport will be on top of the foundation, leaving one row of tile on either side.

Place floor tiles on the second story above your "carport" space, including the overhang over the sides of the walls.

ace columns in the carport
orners; they're not actually
equired but they look nice.

Delete the walls.

This new tool, found under the Terrain and Elevation menus, effectively smoothes out rough terrain. It does this by taking all points within the radius (the size can be changed from very small to very large) and moving them to an average height relative to each other. The highest point in the affected area will still be the highest and the lowest will still be the lowest but the difference between them will be more gradual, smoother, and gentler.

Delete the foundation where you want the driveway. Leave one tile of foundation under each column.

## Non-Rectangular Pools

Can't do this without The Sims 2 Nightlife!

Lay down the main driveway piece.

Want that asterisk-shaped pool of your Sims' dreams rather than those boring rectangular models? Well, wish no more and start digging.

The creativity-limiting rectangular tool has been changed to allow for pools as small as 1 x 1 and has been supplemented with the addition of a diagonal Pool tool.

## Terrain Smoothing Tool

Pools of different orientation can be combined just like decks and foundations, simply laid overlapping each other.

harp terrain can be lowered without making the ground flat and oring with the new Terrain Smoothing tool.

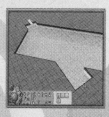

Note, however, that pool objects (lights, ladders, or diving boards) can't be applied to diagonal pools, so every pool that isn't purely decorative must have at least one rectangular section.

As with most Build Mode tools, holding `ctrl` while using the tool erases sections of pool. With the pool tools' new flexibility, however, it can also be used to create islands within pools. If the island is rectangular, it can even be adorned with a ladder and/or diving board and any objects your Sims don't mind swimming a bit to use (why not grill in the middle of the pool?).

To build an island, hold `ctrl` to "demolish" an area within the pool.

## Lot Bin Changes

Unoccupied houses placed in the Lots and Houses Bin can now be infinitely reproduced. When you place a lot from this bin, the original remains in the bin for placement again and again.

Placing an unoccupied lot from the Lots and Houses Bin no longer removes the lot from the bin. Instead, it remains as a template that you can place as many times as you wish.

Occupied lots, however, do not share this ability placing them once deletes them from the bin.

To remove an unoccupied lot permanently, therefore, you must select it and press the Delete button in the bin's lower right corner.

## Building Under Connecting Columns

You may now build most anything you like beneath the arch of connecting columns. Place a table, a chair, a pinball machine, or a swimming pool if your architectural whims dictate.

## Roof Pitch Cheat

A normal roof

The same house with a 75-degree roof pitch—a bit extreme, perhaps

This cheat permits you to change the default roof pitch of all roofs on a lot to any angle between 15 and 75 degrees.

While in Build mode, bring up the Cheat console and input "roofslopeangle" and the angle you desire. All roofs on all structures on the lot immediately shift to the new pitch.

Floor tiles now cover sloped terrain if it can't be leveled. For example, when connecting stairs are cut into the ground, the adjacent tiles are sloped to connect the stairs to the surface. These tiles can't be flattened without destroying the stairs but couldn't previously be covered. Now, you'll find that they can.

## Sloped Flooring

Floor tiles now cover sloping terrain when it can't be otherwise leveled.

## New Walls and Floors

*The Sims 2 Nightlife* contains more than 300 new wall and floor covering styles.

## New Build Mode Objects

| Objects | Purchase Price | Initial Depreciation | Daily Depreciation | Depreciation Limit |
|---|---|---|---|---|
| Creaky Branches Designer Tree | $215 | $32 | $22 | $86 |
| Driveway—Brick | $200 | $30 | $20 | $80 |
| Driveway—Concrete | $150 | $23 | $15 | $60 |
| Driveway Extension Piece—Brick | $350 | $53 | $35 | $140 |
| Driveway Extension Piece—Concrete | $300 | $45 | $30 | $120 |
| Easy Swing Door | $250 | $15 | $10 | $40 |
| Gone Legit by The Family Furnishings | $95 | $15 | $10 | $40 |
| Hartford Connecting Arched Column | $120 | $0 | $0 | $0 |
| OpenAuto Garage Door | $600 | $90 | $60 | $240 |
| OpenMe Arch | $220 | $34 | $23 | $92 |
| OpenMe Door | $225 | $15 | $10 | $40 |
| OpenMe Window | $90 | $13 | $9 | $36 |
| OpenMe Window Wide | $210 | $30 | $20 | $80 |
| The Sentry by WroughtCo | $190 | $28 | $19 | $76 |

# The Sims 2 Nightlife Expansion Pack

## Chapter 12

# Downtown

## A Tour of Downtown

### Community Lots

Each of the profiles listed below details the activities and services your Sim will find upon arriving.

### Bernard's Botanical Dining

♦ Attractions: Restaurant, photo booth, swing set, chess board, darts, bubble blower

### Cold Issue Clothing

♦ Attractions: Clothes shopping, magazine shopping, cologne shopping, clothing booths, grill, gadget kiosk

### Comandgo Emporium

♦ Attractions: Grill, clothing shopping, video game shopping, clothing booth, cologne shopping, TV

### Crypt O' Night Club

♦ Attractions: Pinball, dance spheres, DJ booth, photo booth, restaurant, bar

### Deh'Javu Modern Art Museum

♦ Attractions: Grills, espresso bar, TV, chess

**note**
Be sure to check out the flaming toilet...but don't sit on it!

## FM

◆ Attractions:
Karaoke, restaurant,
photo booth, stereo

◆ Attractions:
Television, bookshelf,
grill, card table,
computer

## Fresh Rush Grocery

◆ Attractions: Photo
booth, grocery
shopping, cologne
shopping, video
game shopping,
grill, magazine
shopping, swing set,
gadget kiosk

## Hans' Trap Door Corp

◆ Attractions: Clothes
shopping, cologne
shopping, grill,
clothing booth,
gadget kiosk

## Go Here Sunshine Park

◆ Attractions: Chess,
grills, espresso bar

## Londoste

◆ Attractions:
Restaurant, bar,
chess, darts

## Gothier Green Lawns

**note**

The town cemetery. Great place to
move tombstones/urns from your
residential lots.

## Lost in Love Hedge Maze

◆ Attractions: Grill,
pool, chess, swing
set, photo booth

### Lucky Shack Cards and Drink

- Attractions: Card tables, karaoke, bar, grill, juice barrel

### LuLu Lounge

- Attractions: Bar, grill, hot tub, DJ booth, dance sphere

### Maple Springs Pool and Spa

- Attractions: Swimming pools, hot tub, chess, cologne shopping, clothing shopping, clothing booth, darts, grill, dance sphere, workout benches, espresso bar

### Midnight Flows

- Attractions: Restaurant, karaoke, bar, jukebox, bubble blower

### One-Twenty-Five Café

- Attractions: Restaurant, chess, darts, espresso machine

### Oresha Family Dining

- Attractions: Swing set, restaurant, chess, Myshuno, photo booth

### P.U.R.E.

- Attractions: Bar, DJ booth, hot tubs, grills, computer, dance sphere

## Red's Famous '50s Diner

◆ Attractions: Restaurant, jukebox, pinball, photo booth, pool table

## Rodney's Hideout

◆ Attractions: Piano, card tables, restaurant, pool table

## Sim Center North

◆ Attractions: Swing set, grills, darts, piano, chess, musical instruments, bonfire, espresso bar

## Sim Center South

◆ Attractions: Grills, swimming pool, Myshuno, chess

## SimBowl Lanes

◆ Attractions: Pinball, restaurant, bowling, pool table

## Similar Sights Sculpture Park

◆ Attractions: Grills, chess, photo booth, bubble blower, espresso bar

## Sims Gone Wired

- ◆ Attractions: Pinball, video game shopping, magazine shopping, chess, bookshelves, computers, restaurant, TV, gadget kiosk, espresso bar

## The Corner Shoppes

- ◆ Attractions: Cologne shopping, video game shopping, magazine shopping, clothes shopping, clothing booths, grills, pinball, photo booth

## Speedy's Fast Lanes Bowling and Eats

- ◆ Attractions: Bowling, jukebox, pinball, restaurant, pool table

## The Hub

- ◆ Attractions: DJ booth, dance sphere, bar, darts, restaurant

## Sugar Cube Bowling

- ◆ Attractions: Grill, DJ booth, bowling, bar, photo booth, pool table

## Residential Lots

### note

All residential lots in downtown are basically furnished and feature at least a driveway for a personal vehicle.

### 103 Custer Boulevard

- ◆ Bedrooms: 3
- ◆ Garage: Detached

## 105 Custer Boulevard

◆ Bedrooms: 2
◆ Garage: Detached

## 107 Custer Boulevard

◆ Bedrooms: 2
◆ Garage: Attached

## 201 Custer Boulevard

◆ Bedrooms: 2
◆ Garage: n/a

## 205 Custer Boulevard

◆ Bedrooms: 2
◆ Garage: Detached

## 31 Mendoza Lane

◆ Bedrooms: 1
◆ Garage: n/a

## 33 Mendoza Lane

◆ Bedrooms: 1
◆ Garage: n/a

## 34 King Street

◆ Bedrooms: 2
◆ Garage: Detached

# THE SIMS 2 nightlife EXPANSION PACK

## 35 King Street

- ◆ Bedrooms: 3
- ◆ Garage: Attached

## 35 Mendoza Lane

- ◆ Bedrooms: 2
- ◆ Garage: n/a

## 36 Greaves Avenue

- ◆ Bedrooms: 2
- ◆ Garage: n/a
- [EBL]

## 37 Mendoza Lane

- ◆ Bedrooms: 1
- ◆ Garage: n/a

## 38 Greaves Avenue

- ◆ Bedrooms: 2
- ◆ Garage: n/a

## House of Fallen Trees

- ◆ Bedrooms: 4
- ◆ Garage: Detached

### tip
Whatever you do, don't look in the basement!

# Building Custom Downtowns

In general, building custom downtowns is no different from building any other neighborhood, but a few options are new with this expansion pack.

Use the Add a Nightlife Destination button to design your own downtown that can be attached to any base neighborhood.

Downtowns, unlike base neighborhoods, are created using the Downtown dialog box that you used to associate or navigate to downtowns. Click on the Add a Nightlife Destination button and select a terrain map just as you would with a normal neighborhood.

The terrain map you choose dictates the topography of your downtown. Don't, however, worry about the type of terrain shown in the picture; you can change that.

Next, name your downtown and select the material for the terrain. Previously, you could only choose Lush or Desert but *The Sims 2 Nightlife* adds two more: Dirt and Concrete.

Give your downtown a name and pick the kind of terrain. You have two new choices: Dirt and Concrete.

 **note**
The Dirt and Concrete terrain type can be used for any kind of neighborhood, not just downtowns.

Once the downtown is generated and automatically associated with the base neighborhood, the next step is to create your lots. There are no hard-and-fast rules as to what goes in a downtown, but your Sims likely expect it to be largely composed of Community Lots. Use all of the existing and new objects to build destinations that can satisfy all your Sims' needs and make for effective outings and dates.

To delete a neighborhood, click on its icon in the Downtown chooser menu to open its detail view, then click on the small trash icon to the right of the downtown's thumbnail. Since you can never delete *all* downtowns, the trash icon will only appear when you have more than one downtown in the chooser.

# Building Restaurants

Though the rules and conventions of Community Lot building apply equally to downtowns, a new ability comes with this expansion pack. You may now build functioning restaurants, but you must follow very strict rules for their basic operation.

For a working restaurant, you need a host podium...    ...at least one table...

If any essential elements are missing, the host podium looks like this.

...at least one chair...    ...and a restaurant stove.

Any lot can be or contain a restaurant; a functioning eatery is not defined by the lot but rather by a set of required objects. To operate as a restaurant, a lot must have:

◆ At least one host podium ("Gastronomique" Restaurant Podium)

◆ A food service stove (Tempest Cooktop from Cuas)

◆ At least one dining table or counter piece

◆ At least one chair

If any of these elements are missing, the restaurant will not function and your Sims won't be able to dine. A nonfunctioning restaurant displays an "under construction" sign on the host's podium and the Host, Waiter, and Chef may be absent. Until the missing objects are placed, a restaurant does not technically exist.

Beyond these strict but simple rules, you can do a few things to make your restaurant function smoothly:

◆ Keep lots of open space around the host podium and never build it against a wall or a 1/2 wall. Sims converge around the Host, so keep things open to prevent traffic jams.

◆ The stove should always have at least two open tiles in front of it (preferably more) so the Chef can work without impeding the Server picking up food.

◆ Keep the entry to the kitchen clear of objects and foreseeable traffic jams. Consider having two different ways into the kitchen.

◆ Tables must be at least one tile apart so the Server has room to move around them.

◆ Build booths around two-tile tables so Sims can sit next to each other and use the new booth socials. Booths around one-tile tables don't permit this.

◆ One Server works seven tables. If, for example, you add an eighth table, you'll have two Servers. If space is limited, consider adding a second podium because it adds a second Server (and Host, of course) to the lot regardless of the number of tables. Note, however, that the increase in efficiency might reduce your game's performance because having more Servers increases the number of NPCs on the lot.

◆ Keep several tables near the Host for easy flow. The Host always seats Sims at the nearest open table, so keep it a short walk for the busy Host.

◆ Build with at least two different ways of leaving the restaurant. If you want Sims to be able to skip out on the bill, there must be more than one way to leave the restaurant area for the other parts of the lot.

# Chapter 13

# CHEATS

**To summon the Cheat window, press `ctrl` + `shift` + `C`.**

◆ **familyfunds [FAMILYNAME] #:** Used in neighborhood view with a household selected either on their lot or in the Family Bin. Insert the family name to be changed. The "#" equals the amount of money the family will have after the cheat is applied. If you want the Tester family with $5,000 to have $10,000, then click on their household or their icon in the Family Bin and input "familyfunds Tester 10000". If you instead want to add or subtract from family funds, type "familyfunds Tester +5000". Either way, the Tester family will end up with $10,000.

◆ **roofslopeangle [15–75]:** In Build mode, adjusts the slope angle on all roofs on a lot.

◆ **showHeadlines [on/off]:** Makes invisible all thought balloons, relationship change indicators (+'s and -'s), and any other overhead headlines. Useful for movie making.

◆ **unlockCareerRewards:** For the currently selected Sim, all career reward objects are available in the Reward panel.

◆ **maxMotives:** Sets all needs for all playable and autonomous Sims on the lot to full.

◆ **motiveDecay [on/off]:** Turns natural need decay on or off.

◆ **aspirationPoints #:** For the currently selected Sim, adds the specified number of Aspiration points to their total. This permits them to get more "expensive" Aspiration reward objects.

◆ **lockAspiration [on/off]:** Freezes Aspiration point decay for all Sims on the lot.

◆ **aspirationLevel [0–5]:** Changes Sims' Aspiration level. 0 puts them in the lowest rung and 5 in the Platinum Aspiration level.

◆ **agesimscheat [on/off]:** Adds "Set Age" to the Interaction menu. Any Sim you click on can be set to any age group you desire.

◆ **setLotLightingFile [filename]:** Change lighting by choosing an alternative lighting file. The original can be found in *C:\Program Files\EA GAMES\The Sims 2 Nightlife\TSData\Res\Lights*. Place your new lighting file in this folder and use the cheat to specify the file name for the open lot. To restore the lot back to original lighting settings, input "setLotLightingFile clear".